ACKNOWLEDGEMENTS

To all the Industry Experts for taking the time out of their busy day, to contribute their advice to my readers.

I would also like to thank God for my blessings.

DEDICATION

To my husband, and our sons, Grant, James, and Daniel.

CONTENTS

1   Your goals and objectives

2   What is a share

3   The Markets

4   Technical jargon explained

5   Publications and Resources to help

6   Choosing your broker

7   Trading Online

8   Research before you buy

9   Getting Started and Buying your First Share

10   When to Sell

11   Other Ways to Invest

12   Summary

Introduction

Welcome to the secret, exciting world of buying and selling shares. I believe it is the most fun you can possibly have with your clothes on.

Who am I? My name is Marie Lewis Stevenson. I have gone from an ordinary housewife to a very successful private investor, and so can you. I truly believe if I can do it, that almost anyone can.

I found myself for the first time in my life at the age of forty-five with the princely sum of £3.000 to spare. I truly did not know where to go with it. Yes, it would have been easy to just tuck it away in a bank or building society. On the other hand, maybe not so easy these days, at least not without the Spanish Inquisition. I searched around the banks and building societies, and the best deal I could find was plus minus a couple of percent. Never having been in the position before of having £3.000 to play around with, I was determined to find a way to increase it by at least 10% in the first year. No small task!

I decided I wanted to buy shares. Why Shares? I hear you ask. Well they allow you to own part of a successful company. Faced with what the bank was offering I felt they would be my best investment over time. Certainly worth investigating at the very least.

I, just like you, set about finding a book for absolute beginners to the stock market. Yes, I found plenty of books, but none that I could completely understand. The technical jargon just threw me most of the time. I am not a stupid person as I am sure neither are you, but some of the jargon was written by experts for experts. I just seemed to get lost in the explanations.

I thought about phoning a stockbroker, but what was I going to ask? I had no knowledge. I thought I would appear to be mad, and would they entertain me with only £3.000? All this was buzzing around in my head.

That was a time ago now. So having had to study this business of shares, I began to gather all the information I required. The only way I knew how. The hard way.

Having gathered all this information and after many people asking how you go about it. I decided to write a straight forward no nonsense book, which gives you step-by-step instructions from what a share actually is, and arms you with the information to make an informed decision when buying your first share.

There are no easy ways to make a million on the Stock Market. It takes time experience and research. That is not to say it cannot be done. Many people have done it.

I have written this book, as I truly believe investing in shares can increase your wealth and grow your capital over time. I believe it is a much better investment than putting your excess into the bank or building society.

I would just like to add here while writing my book I have mentioned some companies. This has been for no other reason than my personal experience. No company or association whatsoever have sponsored my book. Therefore, no other party has influenced the writing of any of it. No party or companies mentioned in the book are recommendations to buy. Remember Shares can go down as well as up.

So, get your coffee or your tea, arm yourself with a notepad and a pen. No, do not think you will not need it. Go on, go and get it. It would also be helpful to have a Financial Times, as further on you can use it to see exactly what I am talking about.

Now put your feet up, and let me help you on your way to wealth through knowledge. Take control of your own financial future.

Above average results, are often produced by doing ordinary things. The key is to do those ordinary things exceptionally well.

1

What are your aims and objectives?

So, you have a little or a lot of money and you want more than the banks or building societies are offering. No shame in that. You do not want to speak to a stockbroker yet because you are not sure what you are talking about. Well you are about to change all of that. This book is the beginning of gaining the knowledge you require to enter the most exciting world of making money. How many times have you wished you could make money by using your brain instead of your brawn? Well let us get to it.

The first thing you need to ask yourself and be truthful is what type of person are you when it comes to taking and accepting risk. Establishing a clear objective here, right at the beginning is very important.

1.   Are you investing for a specific goal?

2.   What is that goal?

Write a few notes in answer to these two questions. Write down your first initial thoughts on what you are trying to achieve. Do you want to retire next year, or are you looking to invest to secure your family's future. Are you looking to enhance your income in your retirement?

As like most things in life, the more speculative investment can offer the greatest reward, but obviously, it usually goes hand in hand with the greatest risk. Whatever your goal is, if you are like most of us, the protection of your hard-earned cash is the number one priority.

Many investors look to shares to provide income through dividends and capital growth. Capital being the operative word for your money. Let us not forget that, in any part of this process.

Before we go much further, it would be wise to look at your current and future financial commitments. Take notes of your answers to the following questions. Be honest.

1. Do you have adequate life insurance cover?
2. Do you have sufficient home and mortgage insurance?
3. Do you have sufficient pension arrangements in place?
4. Do you have sufficient funds in the bank to cover an immediate crisis?
5. Are you investing money you can afford?

The last thing you want, is to be forced into selling your shares to cover an emergency. A smart investor normally keeps a minimum of about three times their monthly overheads for a rainy day/emergency. The money in your shares should be money you can afford to forget about, and sell at a time of your choice.

This is also a good time to mention that shares should never be 100% of your assets. There has to be a balance to your assets, hopefully all earning money. The well-known phrase is true when it comes to investing. "Don't put all your eggs in one basket."

Assuming you have answered yes to the above questions and are comfortable with your financial situation, let us move on.

Risk, risk, risk, risk, risk. You will hear that word a lot throughout this book. What is risk? The true definition of the word is: chance or loss or injury; hazard; danger; peril. To expose to possible danger or loss: to take the chance of. Now knowing all of this, what actually is risk? Would you put yourself or your money at risk? No, of course you wouldn't. Why would you? Risk and money in my opinion are somewhat linked to success.

What risk is there if you stash your money under your mattress? You got it. You could be burgled and lose the lot. A thief could make off with your hard earned loot, as the mattress is a common stash.

What risks are there in starting up your own business? Plenty for sure. If you've ever tried it, you will know exactly what I am talking about. If not, take my word for it.

This is not to say that I don't respect risk, of course I do, and so should you. The smart investors limit their risk or reduce their risk by using many clever tactics. My point is nothing in life is without risk.

There is a massive difference between risk and gambling. When I bought my first shares, a few people commented to me that they thought the stock market was a form of gambling for rich people. Some remarked it was a stupid thing rich people do. Well let me tell you, I know very few rich people that are stupid. I personally would not play games of chance for money. I do however agree buying shares with no knowledge of what you are doing, would be just such a thing.

I think it is safe to say that smart investors understand the risk. Our job is to minimize and reduce our risk through knowledge and information.

Back to the point of what you want to accomplish from your investment.

Growth and Value Investing have been a basic division between investors for years. Who is right, who is wrong. Who knows? There are schools of thought that swear by growth investing and similarly there are schools of thought that swear by value investing. Chalk and Cheese spring to mind here. However in between the two types there is an area of agreeing to differ. It is common for many investors to combine both styles of investing. Myself included.

VALUE INVESTING:

The value investor is somewhat of a bargain hunter. They mostly look for companies with bright futures from a troubled past. They pay great attention in particular to dividends. Don't worry; I will explain in detail what a dividend actually is further on in the book. A company that pays a dividend contributes to your profit as an investor, even if the share doesn't rise. Sounds great doesn't it. I personally find that very comforting. Value investors tend to be very careful where their money goes and tend not to worry too much about short-term fluctuations in the price of the share. Once they've done the research and made the informed decision to buy that particular share, they seem to be quietly confident it will perform well over time. That's not to say they forget about it. Five years is the sensible long-term view in order to maximise your gains.

With all this in mind you might ask yourself, well why would anyone look at any other kind of investing. Well the fact of the matter is they do, and many of them.

GROWTH INVESTING:

Now the growth investor is a completely different breed altogether. They look for highflying companies. The recent share price strength and recent earnings are very important to them. Dividends are not a major factor for growth investors. The reason being many growth companies although not all pay very small or no dividend at all. These particular companies normally re-invest profit back into the business in order to expand or improve. Hence the profits are not paid to the shareholders. Growth investors look for companies that are growing around plus minus 20% per year. I know that sounds a lot, but it does happen. The expectations of investors in these companies are high. Hence they don't worry too much about the dividend. Has a light just come on somewhere? Well it did for me. A growth share depends on its earnings and the acceleration of its earnings, and here cometh the grand word RISK.

Now if for some reason, and there are plenty, the growth company fails to deliver the goodies as in the earnings. Well what happens next? All hell breaks loose. This is the every man or woman for themselves time. In some cases all is fair in love and shares. But let's not go there right at the moment. We are not supposed to get emotional about our shares.

So having showed you the difference between the two styles in simple terms, you yourself now have to decide which suits you best. Or do you choose a little of both? Whatever, or which ever you decide, make the decision and know where you are going. Know what kind of investor you are. It is really important.

I personally have a bit of both. I just love the excitement of growth investing. But I would never dream of having only growth investments in my portfolio.

There is of course as I have discovered a third guest at this party. I have not read a great deal of literature or information on this one, but I am sure there is a great deal of it out there. This appears to be investors just going totally with a trend.

For example. A piece of news breaks about a company and the share price starts to rise. These investors just seem to pile in and go with the trend. They jump back out when they have made a quick profit, or as it turns out, it can be a quick loss. Either way they are there for a very short period of time. They are known, as the trend is my friend. I am led to believe, serious investors do not admire this practise. What happens if the share doesn't rise on the particular piece of news? Well I would say this is one of the riskiest things I have seen regarding investment. I can definitely say this is not recommended for a beginner. Do not think about becoming a trend is my friend person. This is quite definitely for experienced investors only. Quite amusing though, don't you think?

Now just to recap what you should be clear about from this chapter.

1. Are you comfortable that you can afford to invest?
2. Have you examined your finances thoroughly?
3. Have you taken on and understand the word risk?
4. Have you defined your aims and objectives?
5. Do you know exactly what you expect from your investment?
6. Very importantly, have you decided what kind of investor you are?
7. Have you allocated a set amount of money to invest?

All of the above questions should be answered with a YES. If there are any not sure, or maybe answers, then take another look and consider if you are ready to invest.

The last question may seem a bit strange and you may have answered, well of course I have. The thing is if you haven't set an exact amount aside, you may well start dipping into other monies. This is very tempting. I speak from experience on this one. So have a figure in mind and be strict with yourself and stick to it.

Please be clear on all the questions above before moving on to the next Chapter.

The fun really starts here.

2

What is a Share?

So you know your aims and objectives now, so let's give you some crystal clear information on how to achieve the goals you are aiming for.

Well the best place to start as with everything is at the beginning.

The concept of share ownership first emerged in 1553. An adventurer called Sebastian Cabot founded the first joint-stock company in which public shares were issued. This was to fund an expedition to discover The North East Passage.

There is no fundamental difference, according to Warren Buffet, between buying a business out right and buying shares in a company. Warren Buffet is in many peoples opinion the most successful investor of our time. He is one of the wealthiest people in America today. There are many books worth reading on this subject but I feel that one of the best available at this time is "The Warren Buffet Way" by Robert G. Hagstrom, JR. This is a true story of a man who started with a few hundred dollars of his own and turned it into billions of dollars today. His company is still operational, as is he today. The company are called Berkshire Hathaway and if you don't buy any other book on this subject, treat yourself to this one. I have listed other good books further on.

I digress.

Of Course it would be most people's preference to directly own a company right out. For this permits you to influence the most critical issues in a business: Capital Allocation.

However, the next best thing is to own a portion of a company by purchasing its shares.

What is a Share?

A share is one part of which a company's capital stock has been divided. This entitles the owner to a share of the company's profits. A share is a part of a business. When you buy a share you become a legal part owner of that company.

Sounds simple enough, but I must stress how important this is when you come to choose the shares you want to buy. Always bear in mind; you are buying a portion of that company.

Do you rush out and buy a new house or a new car without examining all the pros and cons? No, of course you don't.

Let's take a major investment like the buying of your first home. What is the first thing you do? Well most of us firstly ensure we can afford it.

Secondarily we would look at the area it's in. This is all perfectly relevant to purchasing a share in a company. The area, as with your new home is very important. What area is the Company in? Is that area a nice area, is it doing well? In share terms we can relate the area to what is known as the sector a company is in.

E.g. The oil company would come under the sector Oil & Gas . I will cover the Sectors a bit later on, but I am sure you get my drift. Let's just take the oil area or sector. You would look at how that sector is doing in the wider scheme of things.

Is it doing well?
Is it a growth area?
Is it in a slump?

Just as the area your house is in is very important, so is the sector your companies shares are in.

Normally the next stage we would go to in a house purchase would be to have a surveyors report carried out. This would assure us the structure and all parts of the house were solid, and put a valuation on the investment for us. Well just the same applies to your shares. You can carry out your own survey, or you can pay to have one carried out for you. This will ensure the company you are about to invest in is also solid and all parts of it. It will then allow you to see the value of the company shares. In this day and age it is very common for most investors to do their own research. The reason being the Internet gives us access to most information available to the experts and analysts. This was not the case in the past. To finish off the relationship between buying a house and buying a share. Just as you have equity in your house, you also have equity in a company. This is why shares are some times called equities. Equities are ordinary shares in a company. I thought it was two different things when I started investing. I don't know why. Anyway I thought that was worth clearing up. So, just as you wouldn't rush out and buy the first house you see. Neither would you rush out and buy the first share you see.

What is a shareholder?

Well to be honest it is pretty self-explanatory.
A shareholder is a holder of shares in a property or company.

What kinds of Shares are there?

Private investors like you and I would normally buy new issue or ordinary shares.
You may have heard the term "Penny Shares." Penny Shares are basically classed as any company whose share price is less than £1.00. They can be as little as a few pence. Some people may think it's great to hold 10.000 shares in a company if they only cost a few pence, as opposed to 1000 shares in a company at a higher value. The rules of purchase are the same, regardless of the price.

You may also have heard the terminology "Blue Chip" shares. This means shares in a well-established company with a high market capitalisation. The name comes from the highest value chip in the game of Poker. Quite interesting, don't you think?

Why do Companies issue Shares?

Well the main reason, just like the adventurer who started shares, is to raise money for a particular purpose.

How Many Shares are there?

Well world wide, there are millions. However in the U.K. alone there are over 2000 company's shares you can choose from. These are known as ordinary shares.

The price of a Share.

The price of a share indicates the investor's views on a company's future. It is also worth bearing in mind here that shares are only ever worth what someone is willing to pay for them. A share could be valued by the analyst at say 100pence. If however the investors are only prepared to pay say 70pence. Then what is the value of the share? It may be valued at 100pence but it is only worth what someone is prepared to pay for it, which is 70pence. Try and remember this, you should bear it in mind at all times.

It is also relevant to know at this time, when shares are bought and sold it's called trading.

So we move on to why we have any interest in shares at all, and that is of course, how we make money owning shares. In the simplest of terms we basically hope to buy shares in a company and profit from them.

How do we profit from them?

Well we hope the company performs and does well and so our capital appreciation grows and we receive our dividends. This is why value investors pay a great deal of attention to dividends.

When you own shares you become a shareholder. That sounds very impressive doesn't it? Well don't expect to go to the company and declare ownership. It doesn't give you the right to take up a desk in the office or join the Board of Directors for a free lunch. No, no, no, no, no. You do not have the privilege of interfering with the day to day running of the business. Although it is very tempting, at times. Wouldn't that be great just driving up and taking the fat cats desk?

Not likely.

Well I hope you have understood my explanation of what shares really are. It is imperative to understand the basics before you part with a penny of your hard earned cash. If you're not sure, go back over it.

We are moving on to the markets next, so it might be time for more tea.

3

The markets

"The market, like the Lord, helps those who help themselves, but unlike the Lord the market does not forgive those who know not what they do!" Warren Buffet.

This is probably one of the most pertinent quotes you are ever likely to read regarding the markets. This is also where your Financial Times will be of great help.

Well let's get to it.

The market is as it says in the dictionary.

A meeting of people for buying and selling.

Now as you will have noticed the heading of this chapter is plural. The reason being there are many meetings of many people for buying and selling shares, all over the world.

I will list the markets further on but for the purpose of our exercise we are going to concentrate on the U.K. markets.

So get out your "Financial Times."

This exercise can be carried out with "The Wall Street Journal" or any relevant financial paper of the country you live in.

Inside The Financial Times you will find a section of the paper headed "Companies & Markets." Closer to the back of this particular section you will find just about everything there is to know about the world markets and financial information. For our purpose, you are looking for London Share Service. It's normally around page 47.

O.K. so you've got it. Right.

The first sector heading you will normally see is **AEROSPACE & DEFENCE**.

Listed under this heading are the companies that trade in this sector. As you will see there are thirty-two different headings there, listing all the different companies that trade under the different headings. This makes it very easy for you to find a particular share in a particular industry.

E.g. let's just say we are looking for BP. Give this a try yourself. I would automatically go to **OIL & GAS**, and low and behold there is BP.

O.K. So it's easy enough to see and understand the sectors. Take a few moments to familiarise yourself with them. Look for what ever sector you work in, or have an interest in.

Now these companies are traded on the main market, being The London Stock Exchange. I am going to give you some other information now, on some of the other main major markets. It is good to know the history and some information about them. You can always impress the life out of your friends and colleagues with it. It's great for quiz nights as well.

Only joking!

LONDON

There are approximately 2000 stocks from the main London Stock Exchange Market. The London Stock Exchange is commonly shortened to the LSE. This is where most U.K and international shares are listed.

I think you will find the following facts of interest. I was fascinated with the history of The London Stock Exchange.

1760
150 Brokers were kicked out of The Royal Exchange for being too rowdy. They decided to form a club at Jonathan's Coffee House to buy and sell shares.

1773
The members vote to change the name to Stock Exchange.

1801
They became a regulated exchange.

1914
The Great War meant the exchange market closed at the end of July until the New Year. The Stock Exchange Battalion of

Royal Fusiliers was formed – 1600 volunteered, 400 never returned.

1972
Her Majesty the Queen opened the Exchange's new 26-storey office block.

1973
The first female members were admitted to the market.

1986
The Big Bang. With it brought Big Changes. They became a Private limited company under the Companies Act 1985.

1991
They now replace the Governing Council of the Exchange with a Board of Directors.

1995
They launch AIM. A market for growing companies. I will come back to the AIM shortly.

1997
(SETS) Short for Stock Exchange Electronic Trading Service is launched. The Exchange no longer provides transferring stock from seller to buyer. That is moved to CREST Co.

2000
They now transfer their roll as U.K. listing Authority to FSA, short for Financial Services Authority. www.fsa.gov.uk/
Shareholders now vote to become a Plc. They are now "London Stock Exchange Plc."

2001
They list in July and celebrate their 200th birthday.

For more information go to
www.londonstockex.co.uk

So that sums up The London Stock Exchange.

I said I would come back to the AIM as mentioned. So if you go back to your FT (short for Financial Times), come on, keep up. Look to the end of the headings. You will see a listing there headed AIM. This stands for "The Alternative Investment Market" It was designed primarily for small companies. It is regulated by the LSE but has less demanding rules than the Stock Exchange Official List. It was launched in June 1995 as a replacement for the Unlisted Securities Market (USM). AIM has established itself as the market of choice for small and fast growing companies. To qualify for the AIM companies do not need a trading record. They are required to issue a Prospectus, produce regular trading statements and disclose price sensitive information to the Stock Exchange. Most importantly in my view, is they must have a nominated advisor. Advisors must be appointed from a register maintained by the Stock Exchange. More than 300 companies now have their shares traded on the AIM.

Now if you carry on forward on the same page there is another listing called OFEX.

I hope I' me not just cramming all this information to you. It is relevant you know about all these markets, it will help you to make an informed decision. Perhaps you see a share in a publication and it says it's listed on the AIM for example. You will know exactly which market that is, and where it came from. You will also know what that company had to provide in order to be on the AIM.

Anyway the OFEX is a slightly different kettle of fish. I personally do not own any shares in any companies listed on the OFEX. This is not for any particular reason. The OFEX is a share trading market, providing a secondary market for unlisted and unquoted securities off-exchange in the U.K. Prices are supplied by J.P. Jenkins Limited the specialist market maker on OFEX. They are regulated by the FSA. John Peter Jenkins set up the OFEX Alternative on 2nd of October 1995. It was subjected to some criticism founded or unfounded in the past. The regulation of this market is much looser than the other markets previously described. Never the less it is regulated. Have a look at www.ofex.com make up your own mind.

I'll now give you an insight into some of the other major markets around the world. You can always use this for a reference. Thanks to technology we can now trade on almost any market, anywhere in the world.

NEW YORK
Have approximately 1,200 equities from the NYSE (New York Stock Exchange) and the NASDAQ the world's first electronic stock market, which lists many of the world's largest corporates, as well as many of the small tech stocks.

FRANKFURT
XETRA has approximately 400 equities from the Frankfurt Stock Exchange (FWB).
These range from the blue chip listings on the DAX100, to the smaller companies on the Neuer Markt and SMAX.

MILAN
Have approximately 300 equities from the MTA, the Italian electronic market, and the Nuovo Mercato, for the more innovative small to medium companies.

PARIS
Have approximately 250 stocks from the Euronext-Paris.

AMSTERDAM
Have approximately 150 equities from Euronext-Amsterdam.

BRUSSELS
Have approximately 100 equities from Euronext-Brussels, including all the stocks from the BEL20 index.

On most broker sites or listings they look similar to this:

LONDON

FTSE 100
FTSE 250
ALL-SHARE
FTSE AIM

U.S.A.
DOW JONES
NASDAQ 100
S&P 500
RUSSELL 2000

AMSTERDAM
AEX

PARIS
CAC 40
IT CAC 50
SBF 120
SBF 50

FRANKFURT
DAX 30
MDAX
SMAX

BRUSSELS
BEL 50

MILAN
MIB 30
MIBTEL
NUOVO
MERCATO
MIDEX

You might wonder why I have shown you some of the other Major World Markets and this is not all of them. If you want more world markets you'll find them in your FT or click onto www.ft.com/markets. The reason I have given you some insight into the other countries markets is geographical coverage is not a problem now. Most of the Internet broking services offer you trading on most of the world markets. But for us at the moment I think it would be relevant to concentrate on our own in the U.K for the time being. I would suggest that anyone should begin in their own country first before trying to conquer the world. Myself included.

So now you have a good idea of what the market is, let's take a look at some tools we use to gauge the markets.

The most common tool used to describe the state of the market is a form of shorthand known as an 'Indice'. These indices measure the performance of a basket of shares. They tell you about the average performance and therefore express the general movements in prices. Each Stock Exchange around the world will have a popular Indice.

In 1935 the Financial Times Thirty Share Index (FT30) was introduced as a general measure of U.K shares. That changed in 1984 to The Financial Times Stock Exchange 100. (FTSE 100) It is mostly known by its nickname now 'the footsie' you will probably have heard at the end of most news reports. "Let's have a quick look at the footsie." The movement in this basket of shares is usually what is quoted.

The New York Stock Exchange is usually summed up using what is known as 'The Dow.' This is short for The Dow Jones Industrial Average. A fellow called Charles Dow created this in 1896. At that time it covered only 12 stocks. It is still the most frequently quoted index in the U.S.A. It now covers 30 of the largest public companies in America. Some of them you will be familiar with like Coca Cola or Walt Disney.

The 'Nikkei' sums up Tokyo

I won't list every index around the world but as I said each Stock Exchange has its own indices. For us at the moment we will concentrate on the London Indices.

LONDON INDICES:

FTSE	100
FTSE	250
FTSE	350
FTSE	Small Cap
FTSE	All Share
FTSE	Fledgling
FTSE	Aim
FTSE	Techmark 100

I would just like to mention a point here in relation to the indices. If you were looking for what is known as the Blue Chip Companies, they would normally be found on the FTSE 100.

If you were looking for a penny share, a good place to look would be the FTSE Small Cap. This has some of the smallest companies on the Stock Exchange. There is also the Aim for penny shares as well. I am sure you get my drift.

I think we should take a few minutes here to talk about the Techmark as listed above.

I don't think anyone would dispute the fact that technology has made a major impact on our lifestyles and business practises. The fact of the matter is a lot of investors are scared of this market now. Why? Quite understandably some of them were very badly burnt when the famous bubble burst in this sector in the past. Thank the Lord I wasn't involved at that time. I think it is easy to understand though, why it would put you off investing for quite some time. At least in that sector.

However, you only have to look at Microsoft the famous software company to see a wonderful success story in information technology. In less than twenty-five years it has grown into one of the four largest companies in the world. True, there are many technological failures and trying to find another Microsoft may seem an impossible task. It is certainly quite a difficult area for novice investors. If you watch it for a while, you will notice there can be great big swings in it. These swings can be up or down. It is definitely not for the faint hearted. I have tried it myself and found my nerves just couldn't really cope with it. Plus I don't want to be glued to my computer screen every nano second of every day. It is not impossible for novices, but not recommended.

Biotechnology companies are also very tricky. They apply modern technology to developing new drugs. Yes, a lot of beginners are lured to this area by the fact that the next company finding the cure for cancer will make you a millionaire. On the downside if the drug fails or the trials don't work out, they have spent millions for no reward. Where does that leave you when you get no warning and you wake up to find your shares have lost 60% of their value overnight. Definitely not for the faint hearted or novice investors. Be warned.

Communications is another area that has transformed our lives. With the Internet and satellite TV. There can be large rewards in this area but most times the larger the reward the larger the risk. This is an area that requires a mass of research and when you start digging you might find it is quite a swamped market place. Over saturated, comes to mind here. Although, I do own some communications shares. It just requires a lot of research.

It is quite common as I said, on the Techmark for massive swings in volatile shares. However, if you fancy this arena be sure to have your wits about you and a crash helmet is well advised.

Moving on to a lighter note. In many discussions on the stock market, you will hear the phrase used **"Bull Market"** or **"Bear Market"**.

Bulls are what are known as optimistic investors. When they say it is a bull market, which means the index is rising, I just love it. I am quite definitely a bull. My star sign is Taurus, by the way. Not that this is of any interest whatsoever.

Bears are what are known as pessimistic investors. When you hear it is a bear market that means the index is falling. Straightforward enough I think. I definitely do not like the bear market. No bear for me, thank you.

In the final stages of describing the markets, I would like to mention Market Makers. They are effectively and in the simplest of terms, wholesalers of shares.

The stockbroker goes to them with your order for shares. Their job is to make a market in a particular share. They make their money by quoting a two-way price.

This involves a **bid**, this is the price they are willing to buy shares at.

It also includes an **offer/ask**; this is the price at which they are willing to sell.

These two prices can vary widely. The difference between the two prices is known as the **spread**.

The spread as I mentioned can be large. It is I think most noticeable if you are trading a share with very few market makers. It can be very noticeable if you are trading penny shares. Definitely something to keep your eye on.

Offer and ask basically mean the same thing. Some sites use the word offer and some sites use the word ask, referring to a sell price.

I pay particular attention to the spread. This can cost you more than is necessary if the spread is too wide.

On my final note in this chapter, I would like to leave you with a quote by one of the great experts in investing, Benjamin Graham.

"Nobody ever knows what the market will do, but we can react intelligently to what it does do."

4

Technical jargon explained

And now, my fellow investors, I hope you still have your Financial Times handy.

This part of investing known as the jargon sounds much more complicated than it actually is. In my case it is definitely "don't do what I do, do what I tell you."

When I bought my first share, I truly had no idea what price to earnings ratio meant. I wish I had studied the jargon. I do not mean to sound flippant using the word jargon because there is certainly nothing flippant about it. Had I known what the jargon meant, I would certainly not have bought my first three shares. I am still sitting with one of them. Yes, you guessed it, an absolute donkey. Oh that is probably too good a description of it at least donkeys are useful. I live in hope.

Now knowing what it means and understanding what it means are two different things.

So back to the FT. (Financial Times) in case you have forgot. Different newspapers use different financial tables and may be set out differently, but they all give you the same information. We are now going to look at reading the stock tables and what they mean.

So please go to the first heading on the first page London Share Service in your FT. This will usually be:

AEROSPACE & DEFENCE.

If you are using a different newspaper, it does not really matter as long as you have the same heading. Under that heading, you will see a list of companies. You are looking for Rolls Royce. We will use this, as I think it is a company we can all easily associate with. Not hat I drive one, but the company is well known.

When you look down the list of companies, you do not actually see the full name Rolls Royce. You will see the name **Rolls-Ryc.** This is the name of the company quite often abbreviated known as the symbol. If you go further down the headings to **BANKS** and let us say, you are looking for "The Royal Bank of Scotland" have you found it? Great, you have found it. That's right, it's listed under **RBS.** That's its name abbreviated, now its symbol. This is important, as you always need the correct name or symbol when dealing with your Stockbroker.

Back to Rolls Royce. The next thing you see after the company name is usually but not always a little symbol or shape. If you go to the end of all the listings including the Ofex, you will find a Guide to the London Share Service. This explains what all the different little symbols and shapes mean in relation to the company you are looking at. For example the little club symbol means a free annual interim report is available.

In the next column to the name is the **price**. All prices are shown in pence unless there is a £ symbol beside them. So for example on Feb 4th 2003, the price quoted for Rolls Royce was 101. That actually in our language is one pound and one penny per share. This is the price of the share now. You will get used to reading the share prices in pence. Obviously different countries quote in their own currency. The prices quoted are normally the closing mid price of the previous day. I hope you remember what the mid price is. If you've forgot, it's the price in the middle between the Bid and the Offer. Oh no, you've forgotten that as well. Don't worry, it's the price between the buy and sell in ordinary terms.

So for example the bid price for Rolls Royce is 100pence and the offer price is 102pence. The mid price is 101pence.

The column after the price is the + or − column. This simply means plus or minus. This is the amount in pence the share price has gained or lost in the previous days trading. If that amount were huge, you would obviously take a closer look to find out why. This is sometimes known as the Net Change column. That's straight forward enough.

The next two columns are linked at the top where it says 52 week. Underneath it says high and low next to each other. The high is the highest price that share has been traded, and the low is the lowest price that share has been traded. This is based over a rolling 52-week period. The high and low prices basically give you a range of how far that share has moved up or down within the past fifty two weeks.

It is also worth noting if a particular share had a high of 500 and now has a low of 30, obviously there is a dramatic difference. This would definitely need some investigation as to why this has happened. Like most of the columns it is just part of the bigger picture needed to make your overall judgement.

The column next to the high and low says **Vol:** This is the trading volume of that particular share at the end of the previous day, rounded up to the nearest 1000. Dashes indicate that no trade has taken place or the data is not available.

The next column says **Yld**. This is an abbreviation of the word yield. Yield is a return on the money you invest. In the stock tables such as we are doing. Yield is a measure of the annual percentage return a shareholder receives from dividends, based on the current share price. Yield as I said before is very important to income investors. It is calculated by dividing the annual dividend by the current share price. This is what your money produces. It is **not** the total actual return earned by a shareholder for a company because it ignores any capital gains or losses from holding the shares. It is also worth remembering it is based on the current share price, which need not be the price the shareholder paid for the share. In our stock table this quote in the Financial Times is for the dividend yield in gross terms (before tax) and what this means for the cash actually received by an individual (after tax) will depend on their tax rate.

Last but by no means least in the stock tables is **P/E Ratio**. The Price/Earnings this is an abbreviation for Price to Earnings Ratio. This is the quoted price of an ordinary share divided by the most recent year's earnings per share. Earnings per share are defined as the profits that are potentially distributable to shareholders, divided by the number of issued shares. The lower the price earning ratio, the better value the market offers. The long term average P/E Ratio is somewhere around 11. The general idea of the P/E is that it tells you approximately how many years you would have to wait to get your money back on your investment.

I think it is important that you get this, so I will give you a straightforward example.

If a share price is 108 and the earnings per share is 6p, its P/E is 18. This is 108 divided by 6 = 18. In this particular example it would take you approximately eighteen years to get your money back. Some investors look for a P/E ratio of around 7 or below.

Analyst use the P/E as a tool. It allows them to see at a glance and compare the share prices of different companies. So I am sure you realise how important the P/E is. It took me ages to grasp it so I hope I've made it easier for you.

Well that covers what all the columns mean when you are looking at the FT stock tables.

So you thought that was it? I don't think so. That just shows you what's in the paper. It doesn't cover all the technical jargon you need to know.

I also remember reading somewhere and it's absolutely true; in this day in age that news as far as the markets are concerned is considered old. Old in relation to live share prices on the Internet. However, not everyone buys and sells shares on the Internet. I also heard a saying in relation to the Stock Market that any news is better than no news. I think that's debateable.

The meaning of news being old is by the time we hear about it, Joe Public that is it's already old. I think from my own experience that appears to be the case. Also on the subject of news. I was listening to an analyst the other day, and he said not to worry too much about scanning the news minute by minute as such. The news on a company is often reflected immediately in its share price. I think this is also true. I certainly have found that nine times out of ten, the news is already in the share price by the time we hear about it.

Here is a classic example of what I mean. I have looked at one of my share prices in the morning. It has shot up by 10%. I start scanning the news looking for information as to why the price has shot up. There is none to be found. Perhaps an hour or so later, I find the headline. The share has already reflected that news before it is out to you and me. This I must add is not always the case. This I believe is because analysts and experts have live time information, which means as it happens. Where most of us have at least a fifteen-minute delay. The experts and analysts also may anticipate the news, as they know exactly what is going on in the relevant company.As should you,if you have invested in it.

So let's have a look at some of the other terminology used.

BID: I have covered this a little in relation to Market Makers, but I think it's important to clarify it completely. The bid is the highest quoted price a buyer is willing to pay for a share.

ASK or OFFER: This is the lowest quoted price a seller is willing to sell a share.

SPREAD: This is basically the difference between the two numbers, and is kept by the Market Maker.

This phrase is known as the bid/offer/spread.

Most share prices quoted are the mid price between the Bid and the Offer.

Since we started you have heard me mention the word Dividend quite a lot and how important it is to a lot of investors.

DIVIDEND: The dividend is the amount of a companies profit distributed to ordinary shareholders. This is why it is very important to look at whether a company is profitable or not.

It is shown as either a percentage of the nominal face value of a share as opposed to its market price. The amount of the dividend is decided by the board of directors depending upon the profitability of the business. They also consider the need to retain earnings to fund future projects when deciding the dividend. Larger companies may pay dividends bi-annually (or even quarterly) and these are known as interim dividends.

If the share is **ex-dividend,** then you do not have rights to the next dividend; it belongs to the seller of the share.

DIVIDEND YIELD:

This compares the amount of dividend you would have received from a share, to how much you would currently have to pay for that income. It is a measure of the annual percentage return a shareholder receives from dividends, based on the current share price. Remember it is based on the current share price, which need not be the price a shareholder has paid for the share. The Financial Times quotes the dividend yield in gross terms (before tax). Among the big companies the dividend yield is a great indicator of how bargain-priced a company is.

(CGT):

This is just the worst part of the jargon for most of us but we better cover it. As you succeed, it will definitely affect you. I would also like to say that you should speak to a qualified Independent Financial Advisor relating to this part of investing. However, I am just explaining the meaning of CGT. CGT is known as Capital Gains

Tax. Capital Gains are the profit you keep after you buy a share and sell it at a higher price. For example if you buy a share at 70p and at a later date sell it for 140p that's a return of 100%. Any gains made by selling shares, can be subject to Capital Gains Tax. This is paid annually.

Since April 2000 you are allowed to make up to £7,200 of net gains annually. If you do not cash in the shares you are not liable. Any losses on other share dealings can also be offset against the gains.

Gilts (U.K. government bonds) are not liable to CGT. I wonder why eh! Although income tax is usually paid on the interest payments. Most dividends are paid net of 10% tax. Non-tax payers are usually unable to reclaim this. Using tax-efficient vehicles such as PEPs and ISAs may reduce the overall tax liability of an income-generating portfolio. This is what we want. That is a whole new subject, however at least you will know what CGT means when you read it.

On all tax issues it is imperative to seek Professional advice.
The society of Financial Advisors
20 Alderman bury
London. EC2V 7HY

To finish off this tax subject, which is certainly not my favourite, I would just like to mention Stamp Duty. This is a Government tax levied on the purchase of shares. The current rate is 0.5% in the U.K.

Another piece of technical jargon you will need to know is **IPOS**. If you watched a movie with Robert Deniro in it, called "Meet the Parents." The young man Robert Deniro wanted to marry his daughter was absolutely loaded with money. He said in the movie to his suitor, "I made it big in **IPOS**." I nearly laughed my socks off. So the meaning of an IPO is important. Not just so you can laugh your socks off at that part of the movie of course.

IPO: An IPO is an abbreviation for Initial Public Offering. It is the first offering to the public of a company stock. Examples of IPOs you may recognise are British Telecom. They advertised on the TV. Radio and in the newspapers. You ask for a prospectus, you fill it in, write out your cheque and away you go.

Not all new issues are available to Private Investors.

Don't rush into these. Sometimes the shares can go down as well as up. They are no different from any other shares in the risk assessment process. The first twelve months can be very testing for IPOs. I have recently purchased my first IPO and I can tell you I was sweating or perspiring, as you may prefer. I shouldn't have been as I had done my homework, but I still found it quite nerve racking. I purchased some shares in South African Telekom. The IPO price was twenty-six South African Rand per share. I checked on April 4th 2003 and thank the Lord they were R30.50. Long may it last?

The point is you still have to do your homework.

I also want to quickly mention another word here. That is
SHELLS. No, they have absolutely nothing to do with the sea. Well I suppose most seashells are empty, so perhaps there is a link.

SHELL: A shell is an inactive company with a Stock Market quotation.

A more dynamic company looking for a cheap entry to the Stock Market can reverse into them. They are commonly taken over by entrepreneurs who inject their own business interests into the company and use the stock market quote to raise equity finance via a series of rights issues or takeover bids.

STAG:

This is what an investor who applies for a new issue in the hope of being able to sell the shares at a profit as soon as dealing starts. I have never tried this. It sounds quite risky to me. Might be worth further investigation, me thinks.

Working Capital:

This is the money a company has to work with on a daily basis.

Market Capitalisation:

This is calculated by multiplying the number of shares in issue by the current share price.

AGM :

You will get used to seeing this a lot and it simply means the companies annual general meeting. This is held once a year to approve the company report and accounts. The final dividend is approved at this time and a vote is taken on any proposed motions or other company business.

Gearing:

I know if you asked an expert they would give you the standard definition of this word in relation to shares. It is a company debt expressed as a percentage of its equal capital. That is its true definition. In ordinary language if the gearing is high then the company's debt is high in relation to capital. So when you hear them saying low gearing that means the company debt is low in relation to capital. I have always just considered it a fancy word for debt. High or low. You will find it easy to remember if you think of that. That is a very simplistic way that I use, but I should help you further to understand gearing. It can be quite a confusing subject as analysts use different terms to mean the same thing as I have found. The most important part of gearing is to look at the debt of the company. This means the total debt including short-term borrowings. The debt position then has to be compared to the equity funds of the business. This allows you to work out a gearing ratio. So, **Gearing = Debt over Shareholder Funds.** This is the easiest way I know how to explain it. I hope you get it.

Hedging:

This is another piece of technical jargon. It sounds very sophisticated when you hear the analyst saying they have hedged. I used to think they had slept in the traps or decided not to buy for fear of failure. It took me ages to find out; it actually just means hedging your bets. It is basically just taking out some form of protection against, or simply limiting losses on an existing shareholding or portfolio. You take up an opposite position in the same or equivalent stock. Kind of like an insurance policy in simple terms. So you're covered if the shares go down. So the next time you're watching Bloomberg and the interviewer asks the analyst if they've hedged. You'll know exactly what they're talking about. They've covered themselves in some form against loss.

Rights Issue:

You will quite definitely come across this in your course of research. Believe it or believe it not, I used to see these two words and just abandon the stock I was looking at. In my ignorance I thought another company was challenging the right of ownership and a massive court battle would ensue. So I used to just run a mile. However as I learned, it means nothing of the sort. It is when an existing plc (private limited company) issues new shares. They are offered to existing shareholders in proportion to their existing holding. So no need to run straight away. Continue in your research and look at why there is a rights issue. Then make an informed choice to continue or not.

Well I think that covers most of the technical words and descriptions you are likely to come across. Knowing these things will definitely help you to make an informed decision. So the next time you pick up your FT or any other financial publication with a stock table, at least you'll know what you're reading, and more importantly you will understand what you are reading.

Well that's about that for this Chapter.We are moving onto Publications and Resources to help you in the next Chapter. Definitely more fun than this one.

So time for more tea I think.

Yes I am a tea Jenny.

5

Publications and Resources to help

Well I hope you got your tea. I did, and I thoroughly enjoyed it.

Information. Information. Information. I believe this is one of the best statements I've ever heard when it comes to investing. "**Information is Power.**" There are a number of places to get information regarding the stock market and investing. I did consider putting a list of them at the back of the book, but quite frankly, it always annoys me when I have to stop reading and go to the back of the book to have a look. I want the information now. I don't want to wait until I am finished reading, then search through the back of the book. So that's the reason I have put it here.

Your notepad will be handy at this point. Of course you don't have to write them all down, but you can jot down the ones of immediate interest to you.

Good information is the key to all good investments. Without it, you would be as well playing pin the tail on the donkey, with the appropriate blindfold on of course. I personally have never been very fond of that game. Information can come in many forms and from many sources. Good information will help you enormously when evaluating your decision to invest.

Company and investment information is now freely available to everyone. Gone are the days when only analysts and experts had access to the required information. The Internet has made life much easier for all of us to collect the information we need. That's not to say it's the be all and end all of everything. Its obviously not.

Don't take all the information you read in publications as gospel either. Go and look for the hard evidence to back it up.

Depending on the size of your investment capital, you may wish to pay for expert advice. You know the saying **"talk is cheap"** until you talk to an expert. This is entirely up to you. Even when dealing with an expert it is always wise to be well informed. You will feel more comfortable when you know what you're talking about.

The Internet being what it is today is absolutely loaded with information. The problem here is you can be swamped. My advice is have a good look around and evaluate which sites you feel give you the best information. There is no point in looking at hundreds of sites that offer more or less the same information.

If you don't have the Internet, that's not a problem. There are still lots of more traditional places you can get your information . It's also worth asking yourself, why haven't you got the Internet? In this day in age it doesn't matter how young or old you are. Perhaps you should look at investing in a computer, before you invest in shares. It doesn't have to be the top of the range million-dollar machine. It just has to do the job. There are plenty available at very reasonable prices.

Provided it has a modem it is very simple to get yourself on the net. With all the different deals available now, you can stay online as long as you want for around £15.00 per month. This way you do not increase your phone bill, and can look at as many sites as you want. I am personally with BT Anytime. This costs £15.99 per month and allows me 150 hours per month anytime of the day or night. I am no great fan of BT; it just suits me, as I like their set up and home page. That's a lot of hours. It may suit me, but it may not suit everyone.

There is also AOL and Free serve offering similar deals. The ones I've mentioned are not the only ones; there are lots out there. Someone even told me the other day Tesco are doing a deal as an **Internet Service Provider**. The short version is **ISP**. I haven't checked this out.

Like anything else, it's worth shopping around. Some of them offer a free trial, so what have you got to lose. The only thing I must say here is be happy with the service you choose.

Make sure it is user friendly, and you can operate it easily. We are all different. Ask your friends and family members which service provider they use. This is always a good reference. If you're a pensioner or retired, ask your local library or community centre if they are running any computer courses, and do they offer access to the Internet. It's never too late to learn.

NEWSPAPERS:

I feel the best place to start is where we are starting, with the newspaper. It gives you a feel for the investment place. Nowadays you don't have to run out and buy all the broadsheet newspapers in sight. Most of our daily newspapers carry an investment section or page. The broadsheets obviously have a more comprehensive look at the world's financial information. You will often find in some of the daily papers or Sunday Papers what is referred to as **"Investor Tips**."An analyst or an expert in the industry normally gives these. While a lot of them maybe very good, you still have to look for the hard evidence to back them up. What suits one investor does not necessarily suit another. Remember what I said; don't take all the information you are fed as Gospel.

The Financial Times is still in my opinion one of the most respected and quality newspapers available to you and I. It is not published on a Sunday. "Thank God" my husband says. I just love it. There is so much information available in it. You can become an information junkie. Even although I use their Internet site www.ft.com I still like to read the paper. Strange woman I am. It really has nothing to do with the fact that it is pink.

It is worth pointing out, although most of the information on the site is free; there is some information you can't read unless you are a subscriber. Oh, by the way the FT costs £1.00. I guess you've gathered it's my favourite. As you familiarise yourself with the paper, you will start to learn how to read the news behind the news. You may see a little snippet of something on a company that entices you to have a look at it. I have discovered a few gems this way. So be aware.

I live in Aberdeenshire in Scotland and we also have a broadsheet called "The Press and Journal." This is also very good as it has a quality financial Section. You will find where ever you live; there will be an appropriate newspaper.

If you live in the U.S.A. you will have the famous "Wall Street Journal." I am not going to attempt to list every single newspaper, but here's another couple in the UK and their web sites.

The Times/Sunday Times
www.timesonline.co.uk

The Guardian/The observer
www.guardian.co.uk

Daily and Sunday Telegraph
www.telegraph.co.uk

Staying with publications, there are a host of quality investment magazines readily available. Most are available through your local newsagent. If they don't have it, ask them to order it for you. I have.

Most of them cost around £2 or £3. You can also subscribe to them if you prefer. Subscription fees vary and sometimes you can get special deals, so try before you buy.

Some magazines are issued monthly, but a majority are issued weekly. I don't subscribe to a great many, only one actually. In saying that my husband actually subscribes to it and I read it. Great for me. Although I don't subscribe to a great many, I do purchase some different ones on occasion. The one that my husband subscribes to on my behalf is "**The Investors Chronicle**." The Investors Chronicle is published every week and is just marvellous for the private investor. It is jam packed with lots of company news, director dealings, and broker recommendations to Buy and Sell. It also has some great feature writers. My favourite is Chris Dillow. This has nothing to do with the fact that he was kind enough to contribute his top three investment advice tips to my readers. Of course not. I just love his honesty.

Anyway it's a super magazine and a great investment tool for gathering information. Their customer services telephone number is 020 7775 62892. If you want a look-see go to www.investorschronicle.ft.com they also carry items relating to Investment Clubs.

Investment Clubs are also a good way to invest. Sometimes people feel better investing as a group. Two heads are better than one and all of that. Since I am speaking about investors clubs, it might be of interest to you if you are thinking about a club to go to www.proshare.org this site has a super investors training page, and lots of information on investment clubs. There is quite a lot to these clubs and a lot to learn before you set one up or join one. If per chance you thought you could sneak into one unknown, then think again.

At the end of last year the FSA money laundering steering group recommended that the identity of all members of any investment club should be verified. Not that this is a problem, but it does point out that there are strict regulations and guidelines for Investment Clubs as in any other form of investing. I will give you a few other good sites to look at if you are thinking of joining an Investment Club:

www.proshare.org.uk
www.proshareclubs.co.uk
www.uk-invest.com
www.tdwaterhouse.co.uk

These are just a few, there are many more. Just type in Investment Clubs into your search engine and press go. You will be astonished.

Although as I said I don't subscribe to a great many magazines one of the ones I do purchase is **Shares.** This is similar but not the same as the Investors Chronicle. It gives you a different perspective from other publications. If you want a look at them go to
www.sharesmagazine.com

Another good one is **Money Wise.** They also have there own website. For a look at them go to
www.moneywise.co.uk

I will list a few other magazines and their websites. So take a break and go and have a shifty at some of them. If you are reading this direct from your computer, just click on the links.

Personal Finance Magazine
www.pfmagazine.co.uk

Money Observer
www.moneyobserver.com

What Investment
www.whatinvestment.net

Bloomberg Money
www.bloomberg.co.uk

There are lots of magazines as I have said this is just a few. It's also a good idea to buy them a few times before you subscribe to them. I think I have given you enough of them to get you started. In no time at all, you'll have your favourites. We all do.

There are a number of reference publications to look at but the main one is **Company Refs.** Private and professional investors use this. They cover all U.K. registered and Stock Exchange listed companies. For subscriptions or information telephone 01235 551 751.
You can also visit them at
www.companyrefs.com they offer a free Cd trial to let you see how it works before you subscribe. You've got nothing to lose by ordering the Cd and see what you think.

So we move on to Television resources. My personal choice on the telly is Bloomberg. If you have Sky TV, go to news and documentaries, and then go to Bloomberg making money. Its one down from Sky News. They run twenty-four hours a day and cover every market there is. They also run breaking news along the bottom of the screen. Their prices are live as in they are fifteen minutes delayed from the stock floor. This is just brilliant. They also show you the opening bell on Wall Street, which is around half past two in the afternoon, U.K. time.

I've actually been to Wall Street with my family about ten years ago. It's a marvellous thing to see. It's just like it looks on the telly. They have a superb visitor's area and welcome tourists to have a look. You can see down onto the trading floor and read all the history. You can also buy souvenirs and all sorts from their own shop. So if you're visiting New York in the near future, it is definitely worth a visit. I bought my husband a beautiful money clip from the souvenir shop. Quite appropriate, don't you think?

The BBC also run business bites at 6.15 am, 6.45 am and 7.50 am. It's normally, although not always a fellow called Declan Curry. I did contact him for a contribution regarding advice to novice investors. I am still waiting for a reply. However, we won't hold that against him. MMM-----. He also writes for the Investors Chronicle.

The business bites give you breaking business news and often try and indicate if the market will open up or down. They like most don't always get that part right, but never the less its worth watching. Only on weekdays.

There is another programme on BBC2 at lunchtime called Working Lunch. It's usually on at 12.30 lunchtime. Weekdays only. This is a great show. They cover all sorts of topics relating to investing and financial affairs. Their website is excellent. I like the chap there called Shaw. He is very astute and has a great sense of humour. I guess he doesn't buy shares himself. I am only joking! Check out their website. www.bbc/workinglunch.co.uk

Here are a couple of news services that are also worth looking at. They provide financial and business news.

www.citywire.co.uk

www.reuter.co.uk

So my fellow investor's whether you are on the Internet or not, there is definitely no shortage of information out there. If you want more just type in the word investing or shares in your search box. There are literally thousands.

Remember what I said, don't overload on information. Just find what you require and use it to your advantage.

6
Choosing your broker

With out a doubt in my opinion, this is one of the most important decisions you will ever make regarding your investments. The only good thing is, you can always fire them and try another one without a great deal of pain. But who needs the aggravation. Rather get it right from the start. I compare stockbrokers to plumbers. They charge too much, but whom else can you call to fix a blocked drain. Every man to his own trade and all that.

Well we are getting to the nitty gritty now. So get your feet up and request some peace and quiet.

So we want to buy and sell shares. In order to do that, we require the services of a stockbroker. The thought of a stockbroker can be daunting. It was for me. I was brought up in a working class family and was under the misconception they were some kind of higher beings. Yes, definitely not to be consulted unless you had mega bucks. It was compared to playing golf in my house as a child. Only for the rich and famous. Perhaps if you had a lottery win or the likes. Don't let it daunt you.They're actually really nice people on a whole.A stockbroker is a member of the stock exchange that buys and sells shares on behalf of other people. You will find a list of brokers at the London Stock Exchange members firms. Just click on there website.
www.londonstockex.co.uk
There is also a Trade Association for Stockbrokers. You can get a free list from the Association of Private Client Investment Managers (APCIMS). You can also find them at www.apcims.org

Let's face it; it's not really something you can pretend to be. Or maybe you can? Mmmmm--- Only kidding. Oh! I know you can't kid about things like this. Check it out anyway.

Whichever broker you choose it is imperative to check that they are both a member of the London Stock Exchange and regulated by The Securities and Futures Authority, the industry watchdog. All regulated brokers take part in the Investors' Compensation Scheme, which provides cover up to £48.000 if a firm goes out of business. If you plan to entrust more than this to a broker, ask what extra insurance is in place for you.

Make sure you know what you want from your stockbroker.

In days gone by, this would normally be a specialist based in London. No more my friend. This is like any other service you require these days. Shop around. Some building societies and banks now offer a share buying service. Before speaking to a broker remember it's your money. Don't let any broker bamboozle you with words or jargon. If you don't know what they're talking about, say so.They are there to help you. How can they know your level of understanding if you don't tell them? The broker's primary role is to serve as the vehicle through which you buy or sell your shares.

Competition has brought the cost of brokerage services down. Internet online dealing services are constantly applying pressure to the cost per trade.

There are several different types of stock broking services. There's a simple rule here that's easy to understand. The more services you ask your broker for, the more money it will cost. It's like going to the car wash. If you want a wash and go, you pay a nominal fee. On the other hand if you want the super wash, wheel scrub, and the hot wax, of course you pay extra. My husband always goes for the full selection. I am a wash and go type girl myself.

Anyway that has absolutely nothing to do with broker services, but I think you get the picture.

We can put the brokers into three main categories. They are as follows:

Discretionary Brokers

They provide as many services as possible to their Investors.

1. Guidance and Advice
2. Access to research
3. Make investment decisions for you
4. Help you achieve your investment goals

Discretionary brokers are less in demand today, as technology appears to be taking over. The thing to bear in mind here is this broker buys sells and manages your investments completely. He does not require your authority for each deal he makes. Therefore he can buy and sell whatever investments he deems appropriate for your portfolio. Do I hear an alarm bell ringing here? Well that's not necessarily the case. Full service brokers are still used by some people. A discretionary broker is really only suitable for people with large amounts of money. Typically around £50.000. There charges are the most expensive of all three brokerage services. Obviously they do all the work and make all the decisions. They are suitable for people with a large amount of money who don't want to be involved with the decision making of buying and selling.

Well this definitely sounds like a great job. Seems to me, they get to have all the fun with your money and you get to pay handsomely for the privilege.

That's not to say it's not for you. So have a think about it. We all have different needs.

Advisory Brokers

1. These particular brokers will let you buy and sell whatever shares you want. However they will offer advice.
2. They will only carry out transactions with your permission.

3. Many of them impose a minimum portfolio value of around £20.000. Not all of them I must add.

The advisory broker is somewhat half way between the other two broker services. An advisory broker normally makes his money by charging you an annual fee, plus so much per trade. Alternately they may increase their commission charges per trade in order to cover the advisory cost. Well as you can see the amount of money required to invest using the last two brokers is reasonably hefty. I think so anyway. Well, for an ordinary person that is. However the point is there are fees attached to the advisory broker as well. At least you get to make your own decisions. Plus they do give you advice as to whether your decision to purchase or sell a particular investment is appropriate or not.
That's something isn't it?

Execution Only Brokers

Well this does exactly what it says on the tin. These brokers execute only. They offer no advice, no frills, no knobs dials or bells with this lot. They carry out your explicit instructions. In a nutshell they do exactly what they are told. Nice this one isn't it? I like this one a lot. Well that's just my humble opinion. There are obviously great advantages and disadvantages to all broker services. Execution brokers are sometimes called discount brokers. They sometimes don't even get that title. I have known them to be referred to as a share dealing service. The reason being, they're the cheapest of all three services. A lot of online brokers are execution only. If you don't have the Internet, you can also trade by phone. With this type of broker you do all your own research. You make all your own decisions and last but by no means least; you carry your own can. The buck stops with you. I hope I haven't sent your blood pressure up with that statement.

The advantages of discount brokers are:

1. Lower costs

2. Unbiased Service
3. Access to information

Disadvantages:

No Guidance

In my opinion with execution only, the advantages outweigh the disadvantages three to one. This is just my opinion. There are conventional execution only brokers that are not on the Internet, but the vast majority of them are.

Some of the larger brokerage firms offer all three services. You can choose which one suits you. Don't assume because the firm is a big name it will not offer execution only. Most of them do offer a range of services.

The broker service you choose out of the above three is entirely up to you. Did you think I would tell which broker service to use? Not likely. As I've said all through the book. We are all different with different needs and requirements. You have to weigh up your level of knowledge, the size of your investment, and how much work you are prepared to do yourself. That's something only you can work out. However I do hope my book allows you to gain the knowledge you require in order to make your own informed decisions about what shares to buy, and how to buy them.

For a lot of people it's a question of cost. By the end of the book I hope you feel confident enough to manage your own affairs. That being the case, execution only brokers are definitely the way to go. This is without doubt the cheapest form of brokerage. They charge anywhere from £10.00 to £17.50 per trade. This means if you instruct them to buy say 5.000 of the **"I Love Money Company**." They will charge you a set fee of lets say £10.00 for carrying out your purchase. This is added to the cost of the 5.000 shares, and is payable immediately in most cases. Regardless of what broker you use you will always pay stamp duty at 0.5% of the value of your purchase. As I said earlier, this goes to the government and is not an option.

I think it would be a good idea here to give you an example of what I'm talking about. This will help you calculate the entire cost of a purchase.

I LOVE MONEY COMPANY ORD

BUY

QUANTITY	**5000**
PRICE	**0.1010**
CONSIDERATION	**505.00GBP**
STAMP DUTY	**2.53GBP**
COMMISSION	**10.00GBP**
NET TOTAL DUE	**517.53GBP**

The example shown above is part of a contract note from an execution only broker. However, it allows you to see the total cost of your purchase. The price of the shares is only £505.00. You have to pay a total of £517.53. All of these costs have to be taken into consideration. Remember, the share you have just purchased has to perform well enough to cover this cost before you can earn a penny.

Some brokers charge in the order of 1-1.75% of the value of each deal. This can be reduced if you are making a lot of trades, or if you are a very active investor. Remember to be clear exactly what charges your broker will charge.

If you are the type of investor who intends to buy maybe two or three companies shares and hold them for a long period of time. The cost you pay per trade is not of such great consequence in the grand scheme of things. A couple of pound here or there in the trade charges is not going to make a great deal of difference.

However, if you're the type of investor who intends to be glued to the live time prices screen every minute of every day and you want to click the button to buy or sell at an exact nano second. Trading every day or every other day. A mover and shaker. The price per trade can make a huge difference. The point is if you expect to be an active trader, your costs can mount up.

There is also no point in having a cheap cost per trade if the services are rubbish. For example it might only be £10.00 per trade but the website is rubbish. The site may be unuser friendly. They may not have a good information structure. They may constantly have technical difficulties. You have to consider all these things when you're making your choice.

Whichever stockbroker you use, please be comfortable with your decision to use them.

When you have decided which broker services you need, take your time while shopping around.

When you get to the commitment stage and ask them to open an account for you, they will take all your details and of course you will need to deposit some money with them. Some brokers will let you sign up on the spot and just let you use your debit card to transfer funds to the new account. Others may require funds to be held in your nominee account before letting you trade. Some of them will not open the account at all until they have their agreement of services signed and returned.

All of the aforementioned will send you a Client Agreement. This outlines the services your broker will carry out on your behalf. Read the agreement thoroughly before signing, including the small print.

Be comfortable with your broker. If you're not sure about anything in the small print, ask them to explain. You are paying them for a service remember that. They are not Gods and are usually happy to answer any questions you have.

When you instruct your broker with your purchase, he will then contact a Market Maker. I have covered Market Makers remember? They are basically the wholesalers for buying and selling shares. The shares will be purchased and you will be issued with either a Contract Note in the case of Internet Trading, or Share Certificates. I will come to this in more detail as we go on.

So, in the mean time have a look at some of these sites and see what they are offering. Don't forget, if you haven't got the Internet you can go to your public library. They usually provide an Internet facility. You can also go to the Internet cafes. There's usually one or two in most major towns. If you don't know how to get online just ask the person running the Internet café to show you. That's what they are there for.

The stockbroker sites listed below are in no particular order. Just have a look and see what you think. You can click the link if you're reading this on your computer.

www.tdwaterhouse.co.uk
www.comdirect.co.uk
www.selftrade.com
www.barclays-stockbrokers.co.uk
www.durlacher.com
www.killik.co.uk
www.natweststockbrokers.co.uk
www.moneyline.com
www.h-l.co.uk
www.pilling.co.uk
www.imiweb.co.uk
www.redmayne.co.uk
www.charles-stanley.co.uk
www.schwab.co.uk
www.mf.com
www.moneyam.com
www.sharepeople.com

So are you google eyed yet? It can be a lot of information to take in. Don't lump them all together. Go back and look in your own time at particular sites you preferred. Some are definitely more user friendly than others. Make a list, score of the ones you definitely didn't like or that were too expensive. This will help you to narrow down your choice. The ones you did like add to your favourites and go back and have another look. I have only listed a few. If you go to any search engine and type in the word stockbrokers, you will see an absolute multitude.

Perhaps you would prefer to use your banks share dealing service if they have one. Some people feel more comfortable using their own bank. It gives them a feeling of reassurance. Have a look at there website and see if they offer this service and how much they charge. Or if you prefer, phone them up and ask them.

Maybe you prefer a broker you know or have been referred to. Check them out. Never take anyone's word for anything. You have the information and you know how to check their credentials. It's all in this book.

I obviously can't list every broker, so do your own homework and find what suits you. The ones I have listed are well known but there are certainly hundreds more that may suit you better.

My list is just to give you a feel for what the sites look like and what you can expect.

Not to worry, don't panic. You don't have to decide on it right now. Were going to have a more in depth look at trading online in the next chapter.

Lord I hope you've got a computer!!!!

7

Trading Online

Welcome back.

So now my fellow investors we move on to trading online. You may wonder why I have devoted a complete chapter to this subject.

It is estimated that 9 million people in the U.K. alone will make personal finance decisions on line in the next three years. I think that's a good reason to go into this in some depth. Obviously the figure doesn't just mean share buying, it includes all personal finance. Never the less, that's a lot of people.

So let's start at the beginning.

In order to trade on line you will require a computer. I am not going into all the different kinds of computers on the market. Suffice to say most new computers these days come with a full package. They normally come with a modem built in. However, if you're buying a computer at the moment, just ask to be sure. The modem allows you to connect to the Internet. We don't require to know the technical side of how that works, and after all who cares. It just works. The modem is linked to your telephone socket allowing the access to the Internet to take place. So if you don't have a telephone socket, I'll be a monkey's uncle. Assuming you have, the package with your computer normally comes with an Internet service provider.

This is known as the **ISP**. I did mention it earlier. Try the one that comes with your computer and see how you feel about it. There are a variety of providers to choose from. BT Anytime. Aol, Free serve. That's just a few. Ask around. What are your friends and family using?

They normally charge a monthly fee, which allows you to spend as much time as you like on the Internet without affecting your normal phone bill. Check the small print though.

They normally come with a built in search engine. My built in search engine is google. www.google.com

You may have heard of Ask Jeeves. These are only a couple of search engines but there are lots out there. Again, see which one comes with your package. They are normally all very good.

So, you've got your computer. You've got your service provider package and search engine. Where do you go now?

Without a doubt, this is the fastest way to buy and sell shares. I believe in the future, 90% of shares will be bought and sold via the Internet. We live in changing times. I also believe the older and more conventional stockbrokers and finance houses that resist this change, will definitely lose out. So if you are one of that group reading my book. WAKE UP!

I personally do all my trading on line so I do know what I am talking about.

Is it scary? Yes.

I asked myself all the normal questions. Most people do. Especially if you're like me, as in old fashioned. Used to be I wouldn't buy a teacup online. I was terrified someone would steal my credit card details and run up not thousands but millions of debt. My husband thought it was hysterical. I actually find it quite amusing now. I didn't at the time. Like they could? I think that's a natural fear. The other thing I worried about was if the computer system crashed. Would they forget how much money I had invested with them? Well most huge banks or corporations back most online broker sites. Read the small print. Check for yourself. You also have a paper contract so you can see what you own. Last and by no means least, they all have back up systems to cover most eventualities.

The part of the site where you actually carry out your transactions has security encryptions. Hey, nothing is infallible. You could buy your shares through your local stockbroker in your local town and he could do a runner. Let's not go there though. So enough of the gloom and doom and what ifs. Life is for the living.

Don't forget, your own bank probably offers a share dealing service. If you're more comfortable with them, use them. Check out the costs first though, and the services.

Perhaps you may have an account with a full service broker or bank already and wish to switch to an online broker. This is simple enough and your new online broker will normally be able to do all the transfer transactions on your behalf. Some of them even offer special deals for clients switching. So remember to ask.

You can access your online broker twenty-four hours a day, seven days a week. The London markets are only open from 8am till 4.30pm Monday to Friday. Outside of these times you can still check your account and read the news. You can place orders to buy when the market re opens. The world markets are open and closed at different times. Depending on which market you're in, you would need to check the opening times. We are concentrating on the London one.

What happens if you can't get on the net at the nano second you want to buy or sell? Well you simply pick up the phone. All sites have offices and you can phone them. They will carry out your instructions by phone. You must have your account details and password to hand when phoning.

When I started investing, I wanted to buy a particular share that my broker didn't trade in. My husband uses a different broker on another site, and his broker did trade in the said share. I didn't want to wait, and request my site to add it to their stock list. So I asked my husband to buy it for me. Not the first time I must add. I am also not sure if that is strictly a correct or legal practise. Oops!

There was a little symbol on his site, which said the particular shares could only be bought by phone. Of course I was hanging over him like a cheap perfume while he was carrying out the transaction. Worrying that he was losing precious time and the price might go up while he was faffing around. You will know what I mean when you start trading. Anyway, my husband was saying good morning and the usual polite greetings, as you do. As soon as he said I am looking to buy whatever, the chap on the other end of the lines tone changed completely. He said and I repeat, "Well I suggest we cut the pleasantries and get on with it." Well I just laughed my head off. He obviously, like myself realised the price could be going up while the chat was taking place. When the shares were bought, he did revert back to the pleasantries. Brokers are serious people. Thank the Lord. I still find that occurrence quite amusing. My husband was completely taken aback and asked me to use my own broker in the future. Or words to that effect.

I've gone off track again.

The truth of the matter is, what used to only be available to industry experts is now in the most part available to all of us. I just love that. To try this out just go to your search engine and click finance. You'll be astonished. Another one to stick in your search engine is investment. You'll be even more astonished. While your there why not type in the word shares. Off you go then, give it a try.

Can you believe it? There are just masses of sites with information out there to help you.

So let's keep you on the Internet theme at the moment. The computer is bought. The phone line and server are in place. The search engine is ready to search. Lets give them a run for their money. Just sit this book by your computer, and try out some of these Internet brokers' sites for size.

Go into their account charges and services. This will also give you a good idea of the charges per trade and other services. On most of the sites there will be a little box saying quote. You type in the "I love Money Company" only joking. You type in the example we used in the beginning, Rolls Royce. Right. You've forgotten the symbol. So did I, but I've just checked. It's Rolls-Ryc. When you press find it or go, it will bring up the current share price. By the way, I don't have any shares in Rolls Royce at the moment. Try it. If you're reading from the computer just click on the links below.

Happy Surfing.

INTERNET BROKERS

www.tdwaterhouse.co.uk
www.comdirect.co.uk

www.etrade.com
www.ml.com
www.igindex.co.uk
www.proshare.org.uk
www.fool.co.uk
www.redmayne.co.uk
www.fastrade.co.uk
www.sharepeople.com
www.stocktrade.co.uk
www.killik.co.uk
www.barclays-stockbrokers.co.uk
www.mybroker.com
www.sharexpress.co.uk
www.h-l.co.uk
www.cheapest-share-dealing.co.uk
www.fastrade.co.uk
www.esharedealing.hsbc.co.uk
www.natweststockbrokers.co.uk
www.hoodlessbrennan.com
www.directsharedeal.com

Well I hope you had good surf around. As you have seen, there is certainly no shortage of Internet brokers out there. I have only listed a few. The ones I have listed are certainly by no means all of them. It gives you a good feel though of how the sites operate and what they offer. You will also have seen how much they charge per trade, and this can vary from site to site.

The charges are not the only thing that's important. Perhaps one-broker charges slightly more than another, but if he is offering you a much better service, you have to think about that. Perhaps one site is much more user friendly than the other. Price matters, but it's not the be all and end all when it comes to your choice. Don't be too quick either to jump in and register for a free newsletter. Be selective whom you give your e-mail address to. Sometimes you can get bombarded with unwanted e-mails.

Well I hope you typed in Rolls Royce in the quote box of the sites you tried. It's a good exercise. Well whatever price and information you got was approximately fifteen minutes delayed. I think that's pretty quick considering.

Most of the broker sites you've looked at are approximately fifteen minutes delayed with their information. Even on Bloomberg Telly it says fifteen minutes delayed.

You can get online live prices, but they can be expensive. Not just yet, me thinks.

The stock exchange supplies this information to the media at no cost to you or I. I guess that's why the pros have to pay for it. I don't think fifteen minutes of a delay will make a great deal of difference to you or me. If you do, you can type in live share prices in your search engine and you will find companies offering these systems and how much they cost. The Investors Chronicle also carries some adverts for these systems, so if you are interested request the information.

OK. Let's say you've seen an online broker you maybe quite comfortable with. Go back into that site and have a look at how your shares will be held after purchase. It's important to check all these things out before you commit to opening an account.

There are mainly three ways your shares can be held after purchase.

Paper:

Not so long ago there was only-one way to hold your shares. That was in paper. This was the traditional way in the beginning, and some people still prefer to hold paper certificates today. Basically when you purchase shares in a company, the register will issue you with a certificate proving you are the legal owner of the shares. When you sell the shares you will return the certificates through your broker, back to the company.

Some brokers will not allow you to sell before they are in receipt of the certificates. The cost of this obviously has to be paid for. Your name then appears on the share register and entitles you to all relevant shareholder information, dividends and annual reports. A few problems with share certificates are they can be lost or mislaid. This then requires paperwork to ask for replacement certificates and this costs money. That can vary from a few pounds too much more. Plus the hassle.

Also when you do decide to sell, you will have to fill out a transfer form. You certainly don't appear to be able to sell in a hurry with this method. However, it's up to you.

I would also like to point out that some stockbrokers do not allow you to trade in certificated form at all these days. You will have to ask.

A lot of Internet execution only brokers hold your shares in what is known as a nominee account.

Nominee Accounts:

These are special holding companies created for the purpose of holding investments on behalf of investors. Your broker or bank operates them. This cuts out the masses of paperwork involved, and the records are stored electronically. Your name does not appear on the share register. The shares are registered in the name of the account operator. Never the less, you are the beneficial owner at all times. You still retain the rights to all dividends paid by the company you have invested in.These will normally be paid to your nominee, who in turn will either hold them on account, or send them onto you.

You must check this with your broker. All relevant company reports will be sent to your broker and not to you. If you want this information you will need to ask your bank or broker for a copy. The commission rates are reduced by this method, as there is less administration involved than with paper.

Also when you want to sell the shares you don't have a delay of filling in forms and returning certificates.

Membership of Crest:

CREST is the Bank of England's new paperless share settlement system. This is a second electronic option. You also retain the legal ownership of the shares in the company in your own name. This way you can have your own CREST account run by your broker or bank. CRESTCo have an annual charge of £10 for personal membership. (At time of publication) This method is not widely available and is often restricted to discretionary and advisory brokers only. Check it out.

You can contact CREST at

www.crestco.co.uk or telephone: 020 7849 0000

You must check all of these details with your broker before opening an account.

OK, so you've shopped around and weighed up all the pros and cons and decided to go with "I will make you lots of money.com" No it's not a real broker site.

What do you do next?

You go onto the site and fill in the account application. If you prefer you can have this sent out to you, but what's the point? You're already online. They will ask lots of questions, passwords and security questions. This is all for your benefit and protection.

They will also ask you to transfer funds. You can do this by debit card direct from your bank. You could also send them a cheque if you prefer. Remember the cheque will have to clear before you can trade. You can also set up a direct debit from your bank. This also takes time and no trading can take place until the broker has the money. It may be different if you are not an ordinary person but for most of us that is how it is. As far as I know they do not accept credit cards, well mine doesn't.

I would like to mention here as you probably know, unless you are on a no interest credit card, and if you are let me know. I mean apart from a special deal or balance transfer story. In my opinion only a fool would invest money they have borrowed from a credit card. This would be a very expensive way to invest. If you take the interest you will pay for the use of that money. Plus your broker charges. Can you imagine how much you would need that share to increase by, in order for you to make a profit? Well miracles are not included in this book. However I could be wrong. Borrowing money to invest is definitely not recommended.

If you don't have a debit card you can normally set up a bank transfer but I have said already, this can take up to four days. That's four days for the broker to get the money, and four days if you want it back.

I originally had a strange type of Electronic card. This was just the stupidest card I have ever owned. Needless to say I changed it. As soon as my broker said they don't accept it. It was gone. History.

The debit card from whichever bank you have is normally the quickest most efficient way to transfer funds. You can also send them a cheque if you prefer as I said. Perhaps you're not in a hurry to get on with it. Whatever method you use, funds will have to be transferred.

I personally don't like to jump in and do everything at the one time. I like to try and test things first. So let's say you have £6.000 to invest. Why not transfer say £2.000. This lets you see how it all works.

When I was buying and selling shares in the beginning, I used to buy and sell say 10.000 at a time. I read somewhere that you don't always have to do that. Such a simple thing. I can't believe I didn't think of it. Basically what it means if you have a share that has performed very well and you want to sell it, but you're scared it will still climb. Why not sell 5.000. Simple enough, don't you think? The result being, you have taken your profit from the 5.000 and hopefully your other 5.000 is still growing. If not you can narrow the stop loss and still sell at a profit. Anyway that's got absolutely nothing to do with trading online either, but it's worth remembering.

Back to the account story. So, you've transferred funds by whatever means suits you best. Some sites let you trade the same day and some don't. Whether you are allowed to trade the same day or not, you will be sent out an agreement form. This usually outlines all the terms and conditions of the broker and his services. It usually has all your account details on it as well. You will normally sign this having read the fine print, and send it back. Some sites will only let you trade once they have received their signed agreement back. Regardless, it's only a couple of days. Sometimes that can be a good thing. It can stop you diving in there with the excitement of it all, and buying a donkey. I don't mean literally of course.

However having read this book I am sure that would never be the case.

So that about sums up this chapter. We're moving on to research before you buy next. I guess you thought this was easy?

Not a chance.

If it were easy, every one would be doing it, as the saying goes.

No tea this time, lets have a wee coffee instead.

8

Research before you buy

I believe you can research your way to riches. I just cannot stress this enough.

Information, information, information.

Let's say you fancy buying shares in our old friends Rolls Royce. Well would it make sense to look at say the "I love Money" Company at the same time? No, of course it wouldn't. So, it's important to concentrate, and learn all you can about one company at a time.

There are three main areas to focus on initially:

1. Is this a simple business? Do you understand what they do?
2. Does the company have a history? Is it a good, profitable consistent history?
3. Does the company have a future? Is it in a dying industry?

The above three statements might sound simple enough but let's take each one in turn.

1. Is this a simple business? Do you understand what they do?

Is it simple, do you understand it?
You don't have to take this to the extreme, and you obviously don't have to be a coal miner to buy shares in mining. Let's say against best advice you were thinking of researching two companies. The first company is "Stagecoach"
(that's a bus company if you didn't know) and the second company is "I love Money. Com" Now depending on your walk of life one may be more attractive to you than the other.

I would go for the bus company. This is not a recommendation by the way, just an example.

Why?

Because I know people get on buses every day and pay their fare. They also pay in cash, and that's a bonus. I know what they do and how they earn their money.

My son used to work for a security company that shall remain nameless. They counted a bus company's money. It was a lot. I mean a lot. We often joked about how much money a bus company could take in. It wasn't "Stagecoach" by the way. Do you get my drift?

I know very little about companies that generate their income via the Internet like, "I love Money.Com". How do they do it? How does it work?

I would rather research a sausage manufacturer than try to learn the computer industry.That's not to say I'am right, and it's certainly not a slight against any dot Com companies. I think there are some great computer companies out there. I just like to understand how companies make their money. I think people will always eat sausages and go on buses. Then again I did tell you I am old fashioned and I do enjoy simple things.

Now on the other hand, my big son's friend is a graphic artist. He is twenty-six years old and eats lives and breathes the computer. He sells and designs graphics for web sites. My son and his friend have grown up with computers and the Internet. They would have no hesitation investing in a computer company or a dot COM Company. Why? I hear you ask. Well quite simply, they know exactly how it works. People have made lots of money from companies that generate their income totally from the Internet.

Lots of people say beware of Internet or high tech stocks after the bubble burst. I think if you treat them as any other company and do your research you can base your decision on the same rules.

The question is do you understand how that company works? How does it generate its income?

I was thinking of researching a particular TV. related company. I have a good idea how they work. I mentioned the particular company to my teenage boys and they just started laughing at me. Of course I asked why they were laughing.

They replied. "Have you ever watched it?" I answered "no." They continued to tell me how dreadful it was. I asked if this was just their opinion, as it was aimed at their age group. The speedy reply was, "no one watches it."

Not to be laughed at, I turned on the TV and viewed the offending company. By George they were absolutely right. It was just dreadful. So I saved myself a whole lot of research and gave them an extra £1 each on their pocket money. Big spender, don't you think?

Now this leads me onto ways you can use your common sense. I was looking at a company that manufactures play station games. I had read a piece of encouraging news in one of the publications about expected sales for this particular company. I also read there had been a slight delay about bringing the product to market. So I duly asked my teenagers, would they buy this particular game as it was hitting the shelves shortly. There reply, "No, they've been too slow."

The "I am quicker than you" company has brought out a superior but similar type version of the game, I was informed. "There last two games weren't that great anyway." The one son added for good measure.

Do you think I bothered with my research?

Absolutely not.

People are people all over the world. I think some businesses tend to forget that sometimes and so do investors. Not us of course.

It's worth considering what you and your family buy. Where do you shop? Why do you shop at a particular store? Chances are a lot of other people will shop at that particular store. Not so long ago, I found one of the large dept stores I had shopped in for years had become too expensive for me. I stopped shopping there. Guess what? So did half of their customers. Their shares dived, changes were made and customers returned. I haven't yet. I thought I was the only person that stopped shopping there. I am sure you see what I mean. If you wouldn't buy a product or service a company produces or offers, why would you buy shares in that company?

Let's say you work in a biscuit factory. Did you know that very few people that work for companies own shares in them? Why not? I ask myself. Who knows more about what's going on in that company than a person working for them? You can see if the products are good. Is the work force increasing? Are the bonuses increasing?You will also hear first hand if they're cutting back, or if they're having problems.Worth thinking about, don't you think? Maybe as a trial run you could research the company you work for? If it's worth researching of course.

Onto the second part of the statement.

2.   Does the company have a history? Is it a good, profitable consistent history?

This doesn't mean it must have been trading for a hundred years. It just means look at the history. What are the figures like in the past? Are their sales growing? Are their profits growing? Is there debt reducing? They are all common sense questions. You don't have to be an accountant to read the figures. O.K. they might be in Millions but you just ignore the (m) beside the number, and do the calculation. Its basic math.

If you're looking at a biscuit maker and their sales over the past three years have decreased steadily. Why would you think they're going to pick up next year?Perhaps they will? Have the profits steadily decreased with their sales? If they have, that's definitely an alarm bell. What's their turnover like? This can be a tricky one. Sometimes their turnover is increasing steadily and looks great but if they end up with less profit than the year before, obviously that's not so good. So, you're looking for a nice steady increase in sales, a nice steady increase in earnings, and a nice steady reduction in debt. Perfect. This is what we want.

Coming to our third part of the statement.

3.   Does the company have a future? Is it in a dying industry?

Well this is fairly straightforward. Would you have bought shares in the gas lamp company just as your house was being wired for electricity? No, I don't think so. You have to keep up with the times. In this day in age with technology as it is, there are definitely few caves for dinosaurs.

Think about where you think this company might be in five years time. Will people still want what they produce or supply? A lot of this is common sense, but even sensible people forget this. Myself included.

So my fellow investors having considered the last three statements, you've got some work to do. Some points to remember. It is essential the company is profitable. It is also essential it has a positive cash flow, and sound management.

I was talking to a friend of mine recently and asked how she was enjoying her new job. She said, "it's ok but my boss is a dummy. They seem to be making plenty of money though." I asked her how they stay in business if he's the top banana and he's a dummy. She replied, "A monkey could run that place."

What did I do? I immediately started researching the company she worked for. Why? You may ask. Well, if it's a simple business and a dummy could run it. Think about what it could achieve if the dummy gets fired. Even if the dummy is running it for a while, it must have good systems in place in order to produce good results. Right. So it doesn't matter if another dummy gets the job, but perhaps a good manager may take over, which would lift that company tremendously. Dummies very seldom last that long. Mmmm! I hope you get my meaning.

Regardless of all of this, your buying and selling decisions have to be based on hard facts. Remember these three strong fundamentals:

SALES
EARNINGS
DEBT

Ok, so you've chosen a company to research. Where do you start? Well I think a good place to start is with the company's annual report. If you don't read anything else.

This is an absolute must. It's like looking through the window of a company and seeing what's inside. A company's annual report is the way it communicates with its shareholders and interested parties. If you are a shareholder you are legally entitled to a copy of the report. If you have an Internet broker and your shares are in a nominee account, you can request a copy from your broker. This is a service you must be sure your broker offers. You don't have to be a shareholder to read a companies annual report. I thought this was only available to shareholders initially, but guess what? We can all have a look.

There are many websites offering annual reports. The best place to start is the company you are researchings own website. By going directly to the company you can save a lot of time and effort. Most company websites have a link that says investor relations. If it doesn't have that, it will normally have a financial link. Oh! Link is just computer speak for button or line that takes you to the particular page. You can download their company report directly to your computer. It is usually in Acrobat reader so you can save it and read it off line, or you can print it and read it in bed. That's what I usually do. Not to my husbands liking I might add.

If the company doesn't have its own website, that may tell you something in itself. Very few companies don't have their own website these days.

Apparently one area of business that seldom has a website is the undertaking business. I haven't put this to the test. Just too creepy to think about.

An alternative website to the company's own is, www.wilink.com Just click on order Annual Reports, and away you go. This is a free service. Yes that's right, absolutely free. You can download, or have the report sent to you. They have their own annual report club. Many of their partner sites are also there via links. This saves you trudging around all the different web sites. I have used this service and it is excellent. Yip, it doesn't even cost you the stamp. I just can't praise them enough.

Company Reports vary in lay out and presentation, but they all basically give you the information you need. Don't be put of by the reading and what may seem like a mass of information.

Once you've done it once or twice, it is actually quite straightforward. Some of them are even enjoyable.

On opening the front page of a Company report you will normally find a table of contents similar to this:

Contents

Directors and Advisors
Chairman's Statement
Corporate Governance
Report of the directors
Report on the board of directors remunerations
Statement of Directors Responsibilities
Independent Auditors Report
Consolidated Profit and Loss Account
Consolidated Balance Sheet
Company balance sheet
Consolidated Cash Flow Statement
Notes to the Financial Statement
Financial Record
Notice of Meeting

Out of this table of contents there are normally five hard information sections. That's not to say you shouldn't read all of them, but you can normally gauge from the five if the rest is worth reading.

Start with:
The Directors Report or Review:

This quite often gives you a good overview of the Company and its future before you start diving into the nitty gritty. It tells you what the company does and what it's been up to. It will generally tell you any significant or financial developments during the year. It also covers information about the group. Quite often an operating review is included and usually an outlook for the future. It is important to look at the future.

Has he mentioned it? If not, why not? Is he upbeat or just bland? All these points are relevant to your decision to buy or not.

Balance Sheet:

The next thing is the balance sheet. What are you looking for? It's like analysing your own monthly budget. Have you got it? Are you not really sure?

Forget you're looking at millions and just look at the figures. This is a financial snapshot at the end of the financial year. I think the balance sheet is very interesting. This records where the money has come from in the business and where it has gone. This is in simple terms of course. You must be careful in viewing the balance sheet with regard to asset values and how they are financed. The figures only record what the assets cost, and not necessarily there equal value. This can be tricky, so bear it in mind.

Let's say a building company has purchased a parcel of land. The land cost £500.000. It will obviously be stated at that price. That land may have appreciated in value in a short space of time. This will not be reflected normally in the balance sheet. This works both ways as in depreciation as well.

Another thing to watch with the balance sheet assets are the accounts are drawn on a company continuing to proceed. Let's say the company is not doing so well and a forced sale may ensue. Of course as in most things when you're forced to sell, you end up with less than you may have hoped for. That's life after all.

I have laid out an example of a balance sheet from a real company, who shall remain nameless. The layouts vary but the fundamentals are the same. The mass of figures may look quite frightening but don't let it faze you. Just get stuck in and look for the sense in them. There are a lot of hard facts in this sheet that will help you make a decision to buy or not. I think the balance sheet is one of the most important pieces in the company report.

Company Balance Sheet

	note £000
Fixed Assets	
Tangible Assets	380
Intangible Assets	19,306
Investments	<u>19,686</u>
Current Assets	
Stocks	255
Debtors	7,616
Cash at bank and in hand	22,134
	<u>30,005</u>

Creditors: amounts falling due within one year

<u>22,256</u>

Net Current Assets

<u>7,749</u>

Total Assets less curre nt liabilities 27,435

Provisions for liabilities and charges <u>2,664</u>
Total net assets

<u>24,771</u>
Very important

Called up share capital	7,997
Share premium account	6,084
Capital reserve	1,198
Profit and loss account	9,492

Equity shareholders' funds

<u>24.771</u>
Very important

The basic principle here or any balance sheet is:
Assets = Funds.

If you look at the above figures, assets and funds have the same figure. Do you get it? This is a real company's balance sheet. If the company is having problems the balance sheet can indicate if they will be able to cope with them.

Different companies use different formats to lay out there reports, as I've said. Never the less if you've got the fundamentals you will be able to read any of them and know what you're looking for.

The next thing we are going to look at is the profit and loss account. This is sometimes referred to as the (P&L). This is not a snapshot of the overall business. This tells you what the company's profit and loss has been over the last trading year. It also tells you the tax paid, what's left for shareholders and how much of it will be paid out in dividend. One of the good parts of the profit and loss account is it allows you to see how much is not being paid as dividend and kept in the company as reserve.

These are hard facts and figures and are very useful in summing up your decision to buy or not.

I think it's worth mentioning here in relation to the profit and loss account the term 'Creative Accounting' No! I do not believe you've never heard of it. Well that's not to say all accountants are creative, but it is worth saying that profits shouldn't be seen as being equal to additional cash generation. There is generally a column for the previous year's figures, which allows you to compare both. You can easily see from the figures if the company is growing or declining. It is more straightforward than it sounds. I am not putting figures in my example of the profit and loss sheet. The example is just to give you an understanding of the general layout and what the headings mean. You can use it as a reference when you look at your first company report.

I haven't explained every heading, as some of them are self-explanatory. If I can understand them anyone can.

Profit and Loss Account

Turnover: All income from continuous operations, acquisitions and any discontinued operations. Basically everything coming in.

Cost of Sales: I didn't get this at first; I forgot that normally you have to purchase raw materials in order to make something to sell. This is direct costs and includes raw materials, overheads, labour costs. Basically everything going out.

Gross profit/loss: If it's a loss the figure will have a minus beside it. If there's no minus it's a profit. I don't know why they don't just put a plus so you can determine this instantly. I guess that would be too easy.

Operating Expenses: This will normally include distribution, administration and selling.

Operating profit/loss: Easy enough.

Exceptional Items: This can be a bit tricky. It can also be laid out differently in different companies. The one I have looks like this:

Profits/losses on the sale or termination of operations:

Cost of reorganisation

Profits/loss on disposal of fixed assets

Profit/ (loss) on ordinary activities before interest:
This is after exceptional items.

Net interest payable:
This is interest paid as well
as received.

Profit on ordinary activities before taxation:
This is profit after interest.

Tax on profit on ordinary activities:
This is the amount of corporation
Tax payable on the profit made.

Profit on ordinary activities after taxation:
Self-explanatory.

Minority interests:
Some companies are not 100%
owned. So this is the share of the
profits due to the minority
shareholders.

Preference Dividends:
These are paid to the shareholders of
preference shares.

**Profit for the financial year attributable to ordinary
shareholders:**
That's you and me generally.

Retained profit for the year:

Profit kept in the company and added to reserves in the balance sheet.

Earnings per share:

There are sometimes a few different items here. In the one I have it is:

Basic:

This is profit to ordinary shareholders divided by the number of ordinary shares issued.

Basically, this is profit to ordinary shareholders divided by the number of ordinary shares issued.

Before exceptional items this is an alternative measure of earnings per share.

Well I hope you got all that. Don't worry too much if you didn't right now. You can always refer back to it.

The important things you are looking for are turnover and growth.

You're also looking at acquisitions made and how they will fit into the company. Will they be a drain or a Contribution?

You obviously have to look closely at the Gross profit margin. Let's say the company is generating millions of turnover but they only end up with say a 5% profit. Would you think that was good? No, neither would I.

However, here's the strangest thing you'll discover when you start reading company Reports. Some of these large companies run at millions of pounds loss. I couldn't believe it. If it was your local corner store or the village butcher. They would be long gone. However like most things they don't run at a loss forever. Mmmmm!

Well we're not finished yet. The next thing in the company report we're looking at is the cash flow statement. This sets out the movements in cash during the accounting year. It is not like profits. It is almost impossible to create cash out of thin air.

I hope you haven't fainted. I promise it does get easier. This is probably the toughest chapter, but believe you me well worth the effort. The cash flow statement allows you to determine if the company is making cash or just eating it. Isn't that what we are all studying in order to produce more of? Don't forget companies need cash too. They can't buy their tea and coffee with fresh air either. Neither can their workers. So cash is a major player in any company. Ok, here we go.

Cash flow statement:

Net cash inflow (outflow) from operating activities:

Cash effects from transactions relating to the operating activities.

Returns on investment and servicing of finance:

This includes interest and dividends received and interest and preference dividends paid. Servicing of finance is an accounting terminology for paying for debt. It's similar to most of us with our credit cards, but on a much larger scale. Credit costs money that's a fact. Don't you know!

Taxation:

This is U.K. and overseas corporation tax paid or repaid.

Capital Expenditure and financial investment:

This includes the buying or selling of fixed assets and the buying or selling of investments amongst other things.

Acquisitions and disposals;

Cash relating to the buying or selling of business undertakings.

Equity Dividends paid:

Dividends paid to ordinary shareholders like you and me.

Management of liquid resources:

This usually includes the buying and selling of short-term investments. Also withdrawals and payments into short term deposits.

Financing:

Covers the receipts from issuing shares. Loans and payments to repurchase shares and repay the loans.

Increase/ (decrease) in cash:

This is the sum of the above cash flows.

I told you it was getting easier. Just joking! Where is your sense of humour?

The cash flow gives you a good indication if the company is generating cash from its operating activities. This is a far more reliable indication than profits in my view.

Well the last but by no means least important thing to look at in the report is the Auditors report.

Auditors Report;

This tells you if the accounts prepared by the management are a true reflection of the company affairs. It also tells you if all the regulatory and legal requirements have been met. It is worth checking if the auditors report is qualified. Use your own judgement with all the other relevant information.

Apart from the company's annual report there are other research services. Look at:
www.companyrefs.com they offer a free trial Cd.

Another site featuring research summaries and news reports on U.K. companies is:
www.digitallook.com there are loads of sites. I feel you can get overloaded with the amount of information available. So I just use a few sites and kind of stick to them. You're in the business of making money don't forget. Surfing the net all day is fine if it is producing results for your research.

So hopefully you will be able to separate the wheat from the chaff in the company report.

Right. So you have just researched the company you like back to front and upside down. Your decision is almost made.

Oh! did I forget to mention, on top of all that you have to consider, is this a good time to buy? Oh, come on now, you didn't think this was easy did you?

So my fellow investors were moving on to the best bits now. The next chapter is "Getting started and buying your first share."

All that research makes you thirsty, don't you think? More tea required.

9

Getting Started and Buying your First Share

I should give you a warning right at the beginning of this Chapter. Buying and selling shares can seriously affect your love life. Why?

Well once you get into this, it is absolutely addictive. You will find yourself reading everything and anything you can find on the subject. You start studying company reports. Trawling the Internet for information. When the family wants to watch a movie on the telly you'll find yourself wanting to watch Bloomberg. I kid you not. When you're trying to catch up on other things and you just can't justify to your loved one's why you are reading another book or report on the subject.

Just do what I do, take it to bed. When your partners asleep, you can get fired into the reading matter. You might however find yourself pretending to be asleep quicker, in hope that they will just nod off and you can get started on the reading. Never! I hear you say. Well time will tell. I should add however, I am still happily married to my husband and he finds the whole thing quite amusing. He informs me that he is well aware of my pretending to be asleep trick. Only after he read my book of course.

Back to more serious matters.

Before you buy your first share make sure you have a sound knowledge of what you're buying and why you're buying it. Would you buy a car without a test drive? No. I thought not.

Many experts, of whom I am not one, often suggest trying a paper trade exercise. This is basically picking say six shares on a particular day after having carried out all your research.

You then pretend you have actually purchased let's say 10,000 shares of each company. You then monitor the portfolio over a period of time say around twelve weeks. This way you can see if your choice of shares was correct without having parted with a penny. I have never done this personally but I do think it is an excellent idea for anyone that's not confident in the beginning. For anyone in the beginning for that matter. The reason I have never tried this myself is, I think I would be so mad at myself if the shares were doing really well and I hadn't actually purchased them. Especially when I knew I could have. Does that make any sense to you?

On the other hand I would probably be over the moon if they had done badly and I hadn't parted with a penny. I've never been much good at pretending either, so perhaps that's why I have never done it. Never the less we are all different and it is recommended that a beginner would definitely benefit from this exercise. It quite definitely shows you on a practical basis how shares and the markets work.

Picking shares is a little bit like picking horses. Only if you're the type of person that studies the form. If you were studying the form of a horse, would you pick a horse that has never won a race in its life before? By the same token would you choose a horse that was lame? Well the similarity to horses and companies stops there, but it is worth bearing in mind. We certainly are not looking for any lame companies or losers.

Pick a company that has strong fundamental signs as in:

1. **Rising sales and earnings**.
2. **Low debt**
3. **In a growing industry**
4. **Strong Management**

Where do you start when you are ready to pick your shares? Well analyst's tips are certainly better than any you would get from your local butcher or hairdresser.

It's a good idea to purchase a few financial magazines as in "The Investors Chronicle" or "The Shares Magazine."

There are plenty out there; I've just suggested a couple. It is also good sense to start buying and reading the "Financial Times."

Taking the magazines first, they usually have lots of information on what to buy / sell and avoid. Experts in the industry compile this information and you can bet they will know a lot more than you or I. That's not to say they are some kind of Gods. They just know more about it. They don't always get it right either; so don't just jump in on the first one of their recommendations you read. Do your own homework as we have already covered. They are a great place to start though, and they have great analysts and feature columns.

This is where I started. I bought a financial magazine at the train station. I remember thinking, good grief, £3.25 for this magazine. That is expensive. I am a tight fist, I should add.

On one of the pages it asked an analyst what he was buying that week. So I read the article thoroughly, and he gave his buys for the week and reasons for buying. I should add here this was in a bear market.

I discovered then that people buy shares for different reasons. This was in a very bear market don't forget. The three companies were at a price that was lower than their break up value. I had sudden flashes of "Wall Street" the movie. However all three companies were doing badly but they had assets and brands that would generate more than the share price, should they be broken up. I set about my own homework and decided to buy two out of three of his recommendations. Within twelve weeks of purchase they had both risen twenty percent. I just couldn't believe it. What did I do? I held them until they reached twenty five percent and then I sold them. Did I do the right thing? I did the right thing with one of them, as it didn't rise any higher. I certainly did the wrong thing with the other one. That went on to produce one hundred and fifty percent. Can you believe it? This is absolutely true. That was a lesson well learnt for me. Both companies are still trading and have not been broken up. The hundred and fifty percent one is now back on its feet. Oh! And the one I didn't buy, well that is trading today at three times the price he tipped it. You can't win them all eh?

What where the three shares he tipped? Well I guess I should tell you, and if he reads this book he will know whom he is. The first share was "My Travel" The second share was "Bulmer" and the third share was "Royal Sun Alliance" I am not saying this is a good reason to buy a share, but the point is the analyst new exactly what he was doing and made a profit. I did my own research and made a profit from his original article.

Isn't that what it's all about?

I still keep re-investing the two amounts of money from both shares. I call it my speculalation shares money. It has grown somewhat since then.

Most of the magazines that do give you investment tips usually give you the reasons why they're tipping them. They quite often give you another expert's view on that particular tip. They're not always the same.You take that data and then start your own research and make your own decision. The magazines are also great, as you might have been thinking about a company and you see it in the magazine as a **sell.** They might print something out that you hadn't thought of, or you might have overlooked.

You still have to check it out for yourself. Whatever or wherever the recommendations to buy or sell come from, one source is not enough. You still have to gather your own information and data and make your own informed decision.

The Investors Chronicle also carries a few pages titled "Directors Dealings"

Well I thought I had struck gold when I first seen this. I just looked through the listings and looked for the most dealings in the one company, and ran out and bought that share. Can you believe it? What a lunatic. I just couldn't wait for the market to open in order to buy it. I thought this just had to be a sure thing. Why else would all these directors be buying shares in the company? They must know something we don't, or so I thought. I didn't even bother to research it. I was so confident it was a winner.

I sold that share after six months when it just managed to get back to what I had paid for it. Three days after I bought it, the share dived to half of the price I paid for it. I was devastated. I just couldn't believe it. I held on and held on waiting for this fantastic information they must have had. I kept thinking it would bounce back. I convinced myself that anytime now and any day now it would be double what I paid for it. I turned my computer on every day and was astonished it hadn't moved, other than to go down further. The share is still around at the same price today I might add. What a fool I was. Nobody told me directors buy and sell shares for all different reasons. Hence I am telling you my friend, they definitely do. This leads me on nicely to a topic known as:

Insider Trading / Directors Dealings

A little knowledge can be a very dangerous thing.   I have suffered this disease first hand.

Insider buying is in general a positive thing and can help the stock price. The operative word being <u>can</u> and not always. Let's face it if you were the financial director of a company and you decided to buy shares, it would appear pretty obvious you think the company is doing well. This is normally the case. At the very least it deserves further investigation. Fortunately in this day in age insider transactions must be disclosed.

Well let's start with whom an insider actually is. An insider is an individual or key manager or person inside the company. It may be the Chief Executive, the Financial Director or any other Managing Officer. It could also be any member of the board of directors. They all have a first hand view of what's going on inside the company. Insiders buying shares may not be that significant, however if six insiders are buying shares, this could be a buying signal. Definitely worth researching. Although, as I've said, never buy on this information alone.

A similar situation applies to insider selling. One insider selling may be just diversifying his portfolio, or maybe just simply skint. He may want to buy a new house or car and needs the money. Like buying shares in his own company, selling also has many possibilities. Definitely worth a look. However if six insiders are selling shares, this is without a doubt a major alarm bell and should be investigated thoroughly. Even more so and quicker, if you are the owner of shares in that particular company. Investors Chronicle lists director's dealings weekly in their magazine.

O.K. back to picking stocks. It's a good idea to have a checklist. You can use it to see how well the stock you have chosen compares on your checklist. Mark it out of ten.

TOP TEN CHECKLISTS:

* 1   Has the company earned 20% increase per share for the past three years?

* 2   Have they increased their assets and reduced their debt?

* 3   Are they in a good positive growing Industry?

* 4   Has there been insider buying?

* 5   Are analysts recommending the share as a buy?

* 6   Are there any rumours of buyouts or takeovers?

* 7   Are the consumers happy with the product or service the company is offering? Are You?

* 8   How is the company's cash flow? Are they credit worthy?

* 9   Does the company see improving demographics in its own market Place? Do you?

* 10   Does the company have a low P/E relative to its own market or Industry?

See how your stock pick compares to the checklist and weigh up the yes answers and the no answers. It's just a quick guide to how well the company you have selected is doing. Obviously if there are eight no answers out of ten, do you really want to buy that companies shares?

Here is another good idea to try. Talk for 30 seconds on why you're buying shares in a particular company. Do it out loud. It doesn't matter if people think you're off your rocker. I do it all the time. Do you have a good reason? Does what you are saying make any sense.If it doesn't,don't go any further. Choose another company to research.

I think this is a good time to mention diversification. I used to have 80% of my portfolio in the oil & gas sector. Do you think that was wise? Well I did at the time, until the sector was hit badly. 80% of my portfolio plummeted. My whole investment was hit the same day. I quickly learned not to have all my shares in the one sector. It makes good sense to spread your risk in sectors as well as investments. Don't put all your eggs in one basket. It definitely doesn't pay.

I would like to move on to the subject of advice.

Free advice is worth exactly what you pay for it. **Nothing.** I would like you to remember this phrase when your granny's pal or the local coalman gives you a red hot share tip.

A more appropriate phrase is definitely true when it comes to the stock market. "**Talk is cheap**, until you **talk to an expert**." Now I contacted quite a number of industry experts to try and glean from them some advice for novice investors. Many of them just simply ignored me. Some of them were just too busy being busy. What a surprise!!

Never the less to my delight, there are in my opinion some very nice experts out there who really are interested in parting with their hard earned knowledge, to help a beginner.

Embrace this advice. People who have been in this industry for years have given this. It would normally cost you a large amount of money to obtain it. So enjoy.

A big thank you once again to the experts who took the time out of their busy day to give us their valuable investment advice tips. I certainly appreciate it.

Mike Boydel / Managing Director / Money AM Ltd

1. Do not get emotionally attached to your shares, if you want emotional attachment buy a teddy bear.
2. Opinions in the market often cost you money, trade the market not what you think it should be doing.
3. Never catch a falling knife. Falling shares fall fast and furious and take a lot of buying to reverse its trend.
4. Consider the spread (difference between the price you can buy and sell out). If it's large do you really want to throw money down the drain?
5. Do you want to make a small fortune in the markets, well start with a large one!!!

John Glendinning / Chief Executive Officer / Comdirect

1. Make sure you understand what you are doing, and if you aren't sure then don't do it and find out more first.
2. Charges can have a huge impact on the value and performance of all investments, choose carefully and read the small print.
3. Invest in what you know and feel comfortable with, don't just follow the herd.

Chris Dillow / Financial Writer with the Investors Chronicle / previously seven years as a U.K. economist in the city.

1. Understand the risks. Even household name stocks are quite risky. There's a roughly one- in -six chance that shares in Barclays (to pick one at random) will fall or rise by 30% or more in the next year. There's a good chance of gains, therefore, and a good chance of losses. You cannot avoid this problem by researching stocks – the risks remain however much you think you know. There are only two solutions. First, invest only money you can afford to lose, and regard stocks as like lottery tickets – only with better odds. Second, spread risks by holding not just a basket of

stocks, but also assets as well as shares – like government bonds.

2. Understand yourself. Investors waste too much time thinking about companies – only to discover facts that the market already knows – and too little time thinking about their own psychology. But many losses happen because investors make elementary misjudgements. They trade too much, thinking themselves cleverer than they are; they buy stocks just because they are in the news; they mistake random events for genuine news; they get carried away by fads; they are reluctant to sell losing stocks because they hope they'll bounce back. The list is endless. Get hold of a copy of Judgment Under Uncertainty by Daniel Kahneman and Amos Tversky. It's not about investing – but it'll teach you a thousand times more than most investment books. Or read some of the academic papers on behavioural finance at www.ssrn.com

3. Remember – the market is smart, even though most people in it are stupid. Almost all information about share prices is already reflected in prices. It's very rare for anyone to systematically beat the market by knowing more than the market. More often, they just do so by taking more risks. Those investors who do out-perform the market, like Warren Buffet, are famous precisely because they are so rare. Be humble, therefore.

Geoffrey Turner / Chief Executive / Securities Institute

1   To spread your risk, i.e. do not put all your eggs in the one basket, so unit trusts and investment trusts are more appropriate for beginners than buying the shares of three different companies.

2   To know how much you can afford to lose because shares go down as well as up.

3   To realise you cannot beat the market and that in buying ordinary shares you aim to participate in the growth of the market as a whole.

4   Dividends matter. Always look for the ability of a company to pay a dividend.

Timothy P Pinnington / Chief Executive officer / TD Waterhouse Investor Services (Europe) Ltd

1 Educate yourself about your investments so you are not dependant on an advisor.
2 Get a clear, objective understanding of your own tolerance for risk.
3 Don't be rash – take the medium to long-term view.

Chris Evans / Senior Investment Manager / Charles Stanley & Co Ltd

1. First and last rule of sensible investment:

Establish disciplines suitable for your needs and stick to them!

a) If you require a steady income from your portfolio then concentrate on income producing products and shares that grow dividends BUT do not be seduced by speculative areas of the marketplace or investments offering "growth" prospects.

b) If you are looking for growth then historically the old adage "slow and steady wins the race" is usually best. There are booms in oil, gold, and most recently (and painfully) dot-coms but they are speculative bubbles, which can inflict more harm than good to portfolios whereas consistent performers steam on regardless.

c) If you stray from your disciplined path into an area you have not really researched then 9 times out of 10 you come an expensive cropper! The investor must (but rarely) discriminate between investment and speculation. Even the best fund managers admit that the worst investments in their portfolio were undertaken because the heart ruled the head!

On a different tack too many house owners are joining the buy to let boom because "house prices always go up.....don't they?" If they studied the maths at this stage in the cycle they would think again!

1. **Don't buy what you don't understand.**

2. **Don't be afraid to cut your losses if an investment is breaking your disciplines or it is in category 2.**

3. **If it does not look right it certainly is not right!**

4. **If it looks right keep asking questions.**

Well I hope you enjoyed our expert's opinions. I personally gained a lot from them. I particularly liked the buy a teddy bear statement and don't catch a falling knife. I have heard the latter many times and I use it as a rule myself.

When I started writing this book I was a bit wary of asking the experts for they're advice. I thought they might just say no, or just laugh at me. After all nobody's ever heard of Marie Lewis Stevenson, the housewife. Why should they bother? I was pleasantly surprised at how many experts were quite happy to pass their knowledge onto us that we may benefit from their experience. One of the secretaries even asked if I would like a telephone interview. Well I nearly died on the spot. It was all I could do to stay calm and stop my legs shaking at the very thought. I politely asked if I could have the advice written down, to which she cheerfully agreed. I breathed a giant sigh of relief. Why? I have no idea.

Ok, so you've got all this brilliant advice. You're looking at your stock selection and still not sure what to go for. Well let's say we look at our investment as building a house. Remember the old song about the wise man building his house upon the rocks. Maybe not. The moral of the song was if a house was built on the rocks and the rains came, it would not get washed away. If the house were built on sand then it would get washed away. It was a great song. A lesson to be learnt.

Anyway, we are going to build our house upon the rocks. A house of wealth. So what is the first thing we need? You've got it. Solid foundations. We need four walls that will protect us from most things. These will be solid.

You research low priced high yielding companies from the Footsie 100. You may have to start with just one solid wall but that will still stand until you can build the next one. You can get busy mixing the sand and cement to build your next wall while you're waiting. Ideally it is wise to have a solid foundation before you start with the roof or interior. So look at the walls as the companies from the Footsie 100, and the interior from perhaps the smaller companies or growth companies. Try it on paper first, if you're not sure. See how it works. We are all different. I sound like a parrot here.

Ok, so you've carried out your research. Once you've carried out your first research to purchase, you'll develop a pattern you will use all the time. It gets easier with practise.
You've made your decision on which shares to buy and selected your broker. You're just bursting to buy that baby now. Well that's not enough.

It's also worth considering the time of day you choose to buy. In the first and last hour of trading, prices can be volatile. This is especially true with smaller companies. For the first few trades it may be better to stick to the hours of nine till three thirty. Just until you get used to the way it works. Rather avoid eight and after four for a little while. So the time of day is worth considering.

At last you are ready to do it. The big deed. The reason for buying this book in the first place.

Well if you chose a discretionary broker or advisory broker it's easy, you just pick up the phone and instruct them. Don't forget most discretionary brokers and advisory brokers also offer execution only, on their websites.

If you chose an execution only broker then follow me.

I will take it that you have read all the small print. Opened an account. Written down or printed off all your relevant passwords, and transferred your allotted amount to invest.

The next step is to access your broker's website. Type in your relevant passwords and follow the on line instructions.

Most sites have a site map or clear instructions where to click, in order to trade. Most brokers also have a demonstration facility you can select, and it shows you exactly how a trade is carried out. It is definitely a good idea to watch the demo. You'll be amazed how nervous you can become when the talking stops, and the act of buying begins.

I felt as though the stockbroker was actually sitting watching me. I know that sounds crazy but I made such a mess of it. Not just once or twice, but three times. I had to press the cancel button because I was so not sure I was doing it right. I had visions of every one in the stockbroker's office laughing and saying, "Look at this one. We've got a raving lunatic here." I was also scared that a giant hand would jump out of my computer screen and grab me. I was waiting for a loudspeaker to roar out of the computer, "Hey lady, you only get two shots at this, if you don't know what you're doing, beep off." Obviously it didn't, but it can be quite nerve racking the first time you buy a share on the Internet. Don't forget at any point if you're not sure, press cancel. It doesn't matter how many times. Better safe than sorry. No they can't see you from their office. Honest!!!

Anyway so you're logged in. Normally you'll be asked to enter the EPIC code in the quote box. This is the symbol i.e. RBS for Royal Bank of Scotland. Don't worry too much if you don't have the code. Most sights if you type in the first word they will give you a selection of companies with that word in it, and you can look for your company code or symbol.

Failing that, keep a Financial Times at your computer and you can look it up yourself. Anyway, you've got the company in the quote box and you've pressed go. That goes and gets the relevant quote price and usually some other information on that company. You will see the last close price. That is the price it closed at the day before. You will also see the opening price. The price it opened at today. You will also see the bid price, the offer price, and normally the last price paid. Don't forget most prices are fifteen minutes delayed. There will be an option somewhere on the page to click, which will allow you to trade in that share. Quite often some more passwords are involved before your ready to go. You will be asked to click if you want to buy or sell that particular share. You will then be asked how many shares you want to buy or sell.

Make sure the information at this part is accurate. Double - check it before proceeding. When you're happy with the information you have put in, click the go or submit button. The screen will come up with the exact price per share. This is real now. It will also show the quantity you want to buy, how much the stamp duty is, and how much the dealing costs are. There will be a figure at the bottom usually saying:

Total Consideration. That's the complete amount the transaction will cost you. Be very aware before you click the submit button. You only have around fifteen to thirty seconds to take all that information in and decide to submit or cancel. Some sites offer you a refresh button at this point. You can press it and see if you can get a better price. Pressing the refresh button can also work against you as well as for you. If at any point your not sure press cancel. If you just look at it and press nothing, normally the transaction will time out and nothing will have happened.

Don't take the chance. Rather press Cancel. This is the most exciting part of the whole process. You will remember what I've said about nerves when you come to do this yourself. I hope it makes you laugh when you realise you are not alone.

So you've clicked the submit button. You will normally get a confirmation of your order within a few seconds. It's a good idea to print this off. It gives you a double check. You will then be sent a contract note confirming the details of your transaction. If you've opted for certificates they will be sent by post in the next few days. My own broker normally e-mails my contract note, which I print off and keep on file in my computer as well.

When do you pay for the transaction? Well most execution only sites are instantaneous. As soon as you've pressed the submit button to buy the shares, the money comes off the funds you have lodged in your account with them.

So you've done it. Can you believe it? You're actually a real shareholder in a real company now.

Once you've got over the shock and excitement and all sorts of other mad thoughts. It's a good idea to start a watch list. Most sites offer this facility. Just go to watch lists and follow the online instructions. More passwords of course.

You enter the company you have just bought in your watch list and when you log on, you can go directly to your watch list and see how your share is doing. Saves you going to quote all the time. It's a great idea. It's also a great way to see how other companies you were thinking of buying are doing. You can monitor them over a period of time. It all helps in the buying or selling decision. I have twenty companies in my watch list. I use it all the time. I find it a great tool. It does exactly what it says on the tin. It lets you watch how the companies are doing.

So my fellow investors, what comes next?

Well you didn't think you were finished now, did you?

10
When to Sell

Hi there, welcome back. So you've recovered from the trauma of the actual purchasing of your shares. I guess you thought that was all there was to it. Well it's not quite as simple as that. There's still work to be done.

It's a good idea after your very first purchase to start a shares file. This will be invaluable in the future. Start a file for your research work as well. Have a separate file for your buy transactions and your sell transactions. It is also important to keep this in hard copy as well as in your computer. You never know if you will need it.

I guess most of us think our computer will never crash. Well mines did. Two years ago I left my computer switched on with the modem plugged in to my phone line. We had a lightning storm. Well, the telephone line was hit and it travelled down my phone line and bombed my computer. I couldn't believe it. No one ever told me that could happen. Of course, because it is classed as an act of God my insurance refused to pay out. So I lost my computer and everything on it was fried. So I know that has nothing to do with investing but it does make the point that it is always wise to keep a paper form of your investment transactions. Oh and make sure if you have a lightning storm you unplug your modem from your phone line. Or better still make sure your computer has protection against that sort of thing.

Back to keeping records. If you are using a discretionary or advisory broker the same rule applies. Keep your own records. Don't just think because you have a full service broker that you don't need to do this. Don't be a fool and think oh, that's what I am paying them for. Keep records of everything. Errors do occur. No system is infallible. Do it from the very start, it will make your dealings much easier in the future. File as you go. Don't stack it up.

The buying of the shares is actually the easy part. The hard part is knowing when to sell. I know this sounds crazy but ask anyone in shares and they will tell you the same thing. Most of us suffer from what I call the greedy gland disease. Myself included. We always seem to think we can squeeze just another half percent out of that share.

In my opinion if you buy a share and hold on for dear life it can be financial suicide.

Bear markets can kill you in a heartbeat. I have tried this buy and hold strategy, and believe you me; every time I have tried it, I have failed miserably. I am still hanging on for dear life to one or two of them that I keep praying will return to former glory. Why? God alone knows. Miracle required please. No more. I personally will not use that strategy again. I haven't for some time now. I am not saying you shouldn't'. But think about it seriously. You can I am told succeed using this method. I have never managed it. I think because I have been burnt badly with it I am very much against it. Perhaps I chose the wrong shares to do it with. Perhaps it's because I am not a stockbroker or analyst. Perhaps it's because I am not Warren Buffet. Who knows? Who Cares? Use it at your peril!!

Use your own judgement. I always use a stop loss now and stick to it rigidly. No for better or worse for me.

Buying shares is not like putting your money in the bank. You have to keep your eye on everything relating to them. Keep your eye on the industry you have bought the shares in. Keep your eye on world events; they can affect the company you have bought your shares in. I don't mean you have to be glued to your computer screen every nano second, or trawling the Financial Times everyday from cover to cover, but it is important to watch your investments.

I have read the expert Warren Buffet does not even have a computer screen in his office. He is so confident in his purchase; he doesn't worry about the day-to-day fluctuations in the share prices. I think that is just marvellous, but you and I are not Warren Buffet. So watch your shares and matters that could influence them. Stay informed.

There's also a lot to be said for buying more of what's doing well. Say you bought a share at fifty pence and it is growing nicely. Some investment experts suggest you buy more of them. I've never tried this, but it's definitely worth looking at. It makes sense, don't you think?

However back to the subject of when to sell.

Many investors use a system called **STOP LOSSES.** I think this is imperative for beginners. But that's just me. It sounds complicated but it's actually very straightforward. A stop loss is a bit of a safety net. I will give you the easiest example to follow.

STOP LOSSES:

If you buy a share at £1.00. The share price then falls 20% below. 20% of £1.00 = 20p. Your share price is now 80p. If you had set a stop loss at 20%. You would automatically sell this share. This is just an example not a recommendation. Many people set different stop losses. It basically just means you have set a stop loss at the maximum amount you are prepared to lose.

Some investors don't use stop losses at all. I do. It does require a great deal of self-discipline. I feel more comfortable with the protection against a large loss. We are all different. It is definitely harder to sell at a loss, as you tend to talk yourself out of it. You find you start convincing yourself into the fact that the share will come back up. Perhaps it will, but perhaps it will go down further. This is a decision you have to make. Not all shares do come back up.

You may also find if you keep holding a falling share that you can wait forever to see the trend reversed. You've then locked your money into a loser, so start praying, or just sell it and move on. Easier said than done, I might add.

Now if you had bit the bullet and sold at your own stop loss, you could have purchased a different share that may have risen. This could then cover the small loss from your previous error. We all have them. None of us are perfect.

Anyway back to the stop loss strategy. We will stick with the purchase of a share at £1.00.

Let's say your share rises 20%. to £1.20. You would then move your stop loss with it. So if you were working on a 20% stop loss you would now recalculate that your new stop loss would be 96p. Do you get it? The share has risen to £1.20. 20% of £1.20 = 24p. You deduct that from your new price of £1.20 = 96p. Your stop loss always moves with your rising share price. It always moves with the rise, there is no moving it back with a fall or reducing it to suit your mood. If you have the self-control, and you decide to use this system then it is best to be rigid with it. If you are not, there is no point in using it at all. It does work. I use it. It takes a lot of discipline but it removes the decision of not knowing when to sell.

Stop losses definitely cut out the emotional attachment to a share. Believe you me people do get emotionally attached. Some investors actually hold on to losers for no apparent reason that makes any sense at all, other than they've grown attached to the share.

Other investors refuse to sell because their pride gets in the way. They hate the idea that they've done all that homework and research and they've still bought a donkey. A lot of nonsense if you ask me. Swallow your pride, accept the fact that you were wrong, ditch it, and move on. Don't analyse it to death. Life's too short. Shares are a tool to make money, certainly not to lose it. Bear this in mind when you're struggling to press that sell button on a loser.

Different investors set different stop losses and you will need to decide what suits you best.

A rigid stop loss of 10% doesn't really allow for a great deal of movement in the share price. You could find that you're selling needlessly and it's only a short dip before the share starts to rise again. Some people do use 10%.

A loose stop loss would be 50%. This may allow for too much movement in the share price. A further drop from 50% could lose you as much as 55% of your money. Some people also use this.

You have to work out what level of risk you're comfortable with and what level of loss you're prepared to accept. Obviously no one wants a loss at all, but it is better to have measures in place to cover the possibility.

When do you sell a share at all, other than a loser?

Well it's a good idea when you purchase a share to set a target that you expect that share to perform to. We all expect different things from our shares. Once you've decided what kind of investor you are, you should be comfortable setting your own targets for your own goal. When the share has reached that target do you sell?

Well this is a tricky one.

Not long ago I bought shares in Stagecoach. They are a bus company in case you didn't know. This is a true story. I bought them when they were at a real low of 15p. Why did I buy them? Because I knew the history of the company. I knew how hard the owners had worked and built it up from scratch. They happen to be Scottish as well, which is probably why I knew so much about them. I truly believed with all the work and effort over the years, they would not let this company go down the tubes. Anyway, that was part of my reason for buying it. It is also a cash business as you may be aware. Not really a good enough reason alone for buying it either.

I do like to have some speculation money, just for this kind of risky buy. Its good fun. I set a rigid stop loss due to the risk, however Stagecoach started to rise slowly and steadily over a few months. I was just delighted. I had set a target of a 20% rise and I would have been over the moon with that. No small fete I might add. The share continued to rise and when it reached 30p I was just cock a hoot. There was still a lot of negative press about it, and it wobbled a great deal. I had narrowed my stop loss to 2% as I was terrified to loss any of my 100% gain. I sold the lot at 30p.

Now you might think that was the smart thing to do. I did at the time and celebrated walking away with 100% gain. A very rare event I can tell you.

However, the share continued to rise and indeed is at 46p today 7th of May 2003. Did I kick myself for selling to early? No, absolutely not. A bird in the hand is always better than two in the bush. I had made my rules and I stuck by them. Not long after I sold my shares in Stagecoach, I was reading another investment book as I do. Quite the thing this expert said he very rarely sells all his shares in the one transaction. What he does is sell perhaps half at a time. That way he can see if the share will continue to rise, and still have a holding in it. It was like a light bulb coming on in my head.

Stagecoach wasn't the first time I had sold a share and the share had continued to rise. I don't know if I am particularly thick, but I just never thought of selling some at a time. That way you've taken some of your profit and if the share continues to rise, you're still in it.

If it doesn't, you're still going to sell at your hair trigger stop loss. O.K it does cost you the extra dealing cost to sell, but it's worth it. It prevents you from selling a rising star. I use it anyway. Not always, but quite often. I thought I would pass this onto you, as it's not that long ago I discovered this simple gem of information. This simple thing could have prevented me from selling my rising star (Stagecoach).

I digress again.

Back to when to sell.

Here are some of the warning signs of a shares decline.

1. Slowdown in earnings and sales.
2. Reduced dividends.
3. Industry or political troubles.
4. Negative publicity.
5. Consumers unhappy with the products or services provided.
6. Questionable accounting practises.
7. Analysts are recommending selling.
8. Cash is too low.
9. Debt is too high.
10. Heavy Insider Selling.
11. The sudden departure of a Company Director.

This is not all of the warning signs but I think it covers a big chunk of them. If you see anything out of the list above going on with a company you have bought shares in, it should ring a definite alarm bell. There may be reasons behind any of the aforementioned happening, but you should quite definitely investigate at the very least.

Well I think that about covers when you should sell a share. I would just like to remind you if you go for the stop loss system, stick to it and be rigid. Otherwise there's no point in using it. If you go for the buy and hang on for better or for worse, be very aware you are leaving yourself wide open to lose all of your money. I believe even a loose stop loss is better than none at all. Never the less these are decisions you will have to make for yourself.

Remember the old saying **"run to buy stand to sell"**.

11

Other Ways to Invest

Well I had originally planned to finish this book at Chapter Ten. I had intended to leave you with when to sell your shares. I thought about it, and decided although the book is about buying and selling shares, it is only fair to at least cover some of the other forms of investment for you to look at. I haven't gone into great depth, but just given you an insight into what you may have heard of, or will read about.

You will obviously have to seek professional advice if you would like to invest in any of them. You should consider all your options when it comes to investing your hard earned cash. So here are some investments to look at as an alternative to shares.

Exchange Traded Funds (ETFs)

Exchange traded funds are a cost effective, straightforward way of stock market Investment. The objective of the ETFs is to track an index or an industry sector. When buying a share in an ETF you are effectively buying a share in the assets of a fund. The funds assets are usually shares in the companies, which make up the index or sector. I am certainly not going to try and explain all the ins and outs of them but a good example is the iShare FTSE100. This is one of the most popular U.K. based ETFs currently available. The fund invests in securities of the Index itself. The holdings cover a mix of all the available industry sectors in the index from financials to utilities.

The structure of ETFs means there is no requirement to pay government stamp duties. This is a very cost effective way of gaining diversified exposure to the stock market.

They do pay a dividend, which is normally collected by the ETF. They then normally distribute the dividends to the holders of the ETF shares.

For information on this particular ETF go to www.iShares.net they have a button on the site how they work and it gives you a great explanation of ETFs. This is only to give you an example of what exchange-traded funds are, and how they work. Not an invitation to buy.

Government Bonds (gilts)

This is a very popular route for a lot of investors as an alternative to equities. They are simply borrowings by governments, which can be freely traded.

Bonds in simple terms are government securities issued by different governments.

When the British Government needs to borrow money, it issues gilts. They were called gilts as their certificates were gilt edged originally. They are considered to be one of the safest forms of investment.

There are different categories of gilts mainly shorts, medium, long, undated, and index linked. They all offer various redemption periods.

Let's take a short – redemption period up to 5 years. For example, you purchase gilts for £100. and you hold it for the five-year period. The government then gives you the face value. Unlike equities it does not go down. You might wonder what's the point. Well unlike equities varying dividends, gilts pay a fixed rate of interest. This fixed rate of interest is known as the coupon. So let's say you held your £100. Gilt for the five years and the fixed rate of interest was 5%. You would then receive £5 for each year the gilt was held. They pay interest twice a year so you would get £2.50 twice a year equalling £5. per gilt held of £100.

This is only an example but it indicates how they work. It is not just as straightforward as this but if you like the sound of this, contact your broker or financial advisor.

Insurance companies, pension funds and charities who generally want safe high yielding investments, often use gilts.

The return from gilts generally stands a little higher than the bank or building society.

Private investors do not pay tax on capital gains from gilts.

Covered Warrants

Covered warrants offer the private investor the opportunity to gain in falling markets as well as rising ones. I personally feel they are a bit complicated for a beginner but that's not to say you can't investigate them and make up your own mind.

Company warrants have traded on the stock market for years. The underlying company issued them but now the London Stock Exchange has launched a new warrant. This is now called a covered warrant. Financial institutions instead of the underlying companies now issue them.

They are quite often used to protect existing portfolios from adverse moves in the market. They are very similar to traded options. They give you the right to buy or sell an underlying equity or index, at a specified price, on or before a specified date.

Basically if you believe the equity price is going to rise, you would buy a covered **call** warrant. This gives the holder the right, but not the obligation, to buy the underlying investment at a future date and specified price.

Alternatively if you believe the equity price is going to fall, you would then buy a covered **put** warrant. This gives the holder the right, but not the obligation, to sell the underlying investment at a future date at a specified price.

The term covered means in this instance; the financial institution offering the warrant will cover their position with the actual underlying stock.

They are also quite often used to hedge an investment. Kind of like taking out an insurance policy. You may not need it, but you're covered just in case.

They are traded in a paperless format so you would need a nominee account.

They are still considered by most to be a high-risk investment.

Issuers of covered warrants:

SG Securities
Commerzbank
Goldman Sachs
Trading Lab
JP Morgan

A great site for a thorough explanation on these tricky little investments is www.redmayne.co.uk and click on covered warrants. They have a super fact sheet, which you can print of and read at your leisure.

Most brokers can purchase covered warrants on your behalf, but be sure you understand completely how they work before you think about getting involved. Never be afraid to ask.

Spread Betting

I've been let of the hook by a big chunk here. I contacted this very nice gentleman from IG Index who specialise in this field of investing. He kindly submitted this piece on the subject and I am very grateful. His name is Mr Stacey Ash. I would not have attempted to cover this myself. So the following is his welcomed contribution on the subject.

The key features of Spread Betting

Financial spread betting was originated by IG Index's founder (and current Chairman) Stuart Wheeler. Stuart set up the company in 1974 to allow his friends to bet on the price of gold (and therefore not pay any tax on any gains). These friends included the likes of John Aspinall and Jimmy (Sir James) Goldsmith. Stuart wanted to call the company Investors Gold, but this was not allowed by the DTI at the time so he merely shortened the title to IG! Hence we are the oldest such company in existence.

Spread betting may not be for everyone, since it is a vehicle for those with a relatively short-term view i.e. months not years.

However, if you have a short-term view then it can be a more efficient vehicle than normal share trading.

The main reasons for this are:

1. You can go long or short i.e. you can benefit from falling prices as well as rising prices. Therefore you do not need a bull market to make money.
2. You can put guaranteed stops on your position, thereby putting an absolute limit on your losses without limiting your potential gains. This removes the worry of a stock 'gapping' on you if, for instance, it is suspended and opens a lot lower when it re-opens.
3. You can trade on margin. Typically you do not need to deposit the full value of the contract. For example, if you bought £10.000 worth of Vodafone shares you would be asked by the spread betting company to deposit £1.000. You would still benefit from the gains on £10.000 but have had to put up significantly less in order to do so.
4. There is no capital gains tax to pay on your profits.
5. There is no stamp duty on the transaction.
6. You can trade 1000's of UK, US, European and Asian shares on the same account.

These are the main features on spread betting and for further information or more details go to:
www.igindex.co.uk

A big thanks to Stacey for that. They are a really nice company and have an excellent website. Check it out.

Collective Investments

Collective investments work by putting lots of money from lots of investors together and using it to buy shares and or bonds. This is done under the direction of a fund manger. The investors gain the benefits of diversification and the expertise and knowledge of the fund manager. You normally have to pay a variety of charges to take part in these investments. So check it out. The two main kinds of collective investments in the U.K.

are unit trusts and investment trusts. They are not the same thing and have very important differences. There are a huge number of trusts available covering a mass of investment objectives. I have been saved by the bell here as Mr Paul Wynne of TrustNet has come to my rescue. He has contributed the following piece. I think this is a very important alternative investment to shares and it is important you understand them. The piece is a bit lengthy but well worth the reward of knowledge. So get a cup of tea and enjoy.

Mr Paul Wynne / Communications Manager / TrustNet

Unit Trusts, OEICs and Investment Trusts

Summary

Unit Trusts and OEICs (Open Ended Investment Company) are pooled funds of investor's money, which are used to buy a range of shares, gilts, bonds or cash deposits. Both Unit Trusts and OEICs are open-ended collective investments. Open-ended means the size of each fund will vary according to supply and demand. They provide the opportunity to invest in a broad selection of shares, thus reducing the risk of investing in individual shares. Typically, a Unit Trust or OEIC is worth anything from £5m to £300m with many investors, some with as little as a few hundred pounds and some with many thousands of pounds. There are thousands of Unit Trusts and hundreds of OIECs to choose from, so it is very important to select the right one to meet your needs.

When you invest in a Unit Trust you buy a unit, which means a portion of the total fund. OEICs issue shares. The value of your investment will vary according to the performance of the fund. Each Unit Trust and OEIC has its own objective and the fund manager has to invest to achieve this objective. The fund manager will invest the money on behalf of the owners and as the fund grows the value of the investment will also grow. There are strict guidelines for the valuing of these funds, which have to be followed by the fund mangers. You can invest into a Unit Trust or OEIC through an ISA.

Usually, there are no initial charges for having an ISA, and you have the advantage of the investment being tax-free.

CONCEPT

Unit Trusts and OEICs are pooled investments that allow access to a number of shares. They benefit from expert management, and a spread of risk.

Unit Trusts and OEICs are separated into categories so they can be compared against other funds with similar objectives and underlying assets; for example, Japan smaller company funds are grouped together.

The funds can be further broken down according to the risk, returns and length of investment the investor requires. It should also be noted that Unit Trusts and OEICs are generally seen as medium to long-term investment, as time tends to reduce risk.

- Low risk shorter-term investments
- Income and Growth medium term investments
- Long-term saving

Low risk shorter-term investments

These are for investors that wish to invest for a 1-3 year period. Money Market funds (also known as cash funds) are a good way to save money that is surplus to your normal spending requirements over the short-term. They closely resemble bank or building society accounts. If you need to maximise returns, have two or three years before you need the money and are prepared to take some risk then it is worth considering some Money Market funds or lower risk UK bond funds.

Income and Growth medium term investments

Medium term can be defined as an investment held for 3-7 years. Bond funds are designed to provide a good level of income and some growth of capital with low to medium risk. This is because most bonds pay a fixed rate of interest, and though the price of a bond may fluctuate, it generally does so less then a share. You can invest in UK Bond funds, International Bond funds and Equity & Bond funds. The Equity & Bond fund combines the relatively secure income generated from a bond with the higher rate of income, but more risky investment, from company shares.

Long term saving

There are many funds or combinations of funds available for the long-term investor aiming for growth of capital or a growing income plus growth of capital over a period of 7 years or more. An advantage of investing in equities is that over periods of five years or more they usually provide a growing income as well as increasing capital values, outpacing the rate of inflation. Examples of funds that provide income and/or growth are UK Equity Income, UK Equity Growth and Income, International Equity Income and International Equity and Bond.

If you were to invest in UK Equity Growth and UK Smaller Companies funds, the focus of the fund manager would be on growth, by investing in the shares of companies that have a history of good growth. Growth also features in the UK Index funds, that closely follow the shares that makes up a particular indices and Fund of Funds that invest in different unit trusts and investment trusts.

The choices that have been mentioned are concerned largely with sector and not all off the sectors are listed here. Further investment decisions can be found in the region or geographical area of a fund or whether to follow a specific investment theme such as healthcare.

Unit Trusts and Investment Trusts

Unit trusts and Investment Trusts are not the same investment, although they are both collective investments that are dependant on the underlying assets.

A Comparison:

Structure Investing

* Investment Trusts are closed ended, which means the number of shares that are in issue are fixed compared to the number of units in an open ended Unit Trust which may vary according to demand.
* An Investment Trust is a company in itself and is listed on the London Stock Exchange. With a Unit Trust you are buying the underlying shares that a manager will run for you, with an Investment Trust you are buying shares in a company, which invests in shares.
* A Unit Trust is valued according to the regulatory formula; an Investment Trust is valued by the director in line with general accounting practise.
* A Unit Trust is authorised and regulated by the Financial Services Authority (FSA). An Investment Trust is registered under the Companies Act and is subject to Stock Exchange listing rules and Inland Revenue approval.
* A Unit Trust has income and accumulation units only, whereas an Investment Trust has the ability to issue different share classes through split capital structure.
* A Unit Trust is only allowed to borrow up to 10% of the fund, while an Investment Trust has extensive borrowing abilities, known as gearing.

Investing

* With a Unit Trust the investor is holding units, with an Investment Trust the investor is holding shares.
* A Unit Trust investor has to return their units to the fund manager for redemption if they want to sell; the selling of Investment Fund shares is done on the open market and is not given back to the fund manager.
* A Unit Trust has clearly defined rules on what investments can be made, while an Investment Trust is allowed almost unlimited investments subject to the approval of the Board. Investment Trusts are also allowed to invest in unquoted

shares, which mean more risk and potentially higher rewards.

* The price of a Unit Trust reflects the value of investments in the fund (Net Asset Value) plus charges calculated within the spread. The price of an Investment Trust varies according to market sentiment and charges are shown separately.

Both can be bought within an ISA, subject to Inland Revenue constraints.

Unit Trust or OEIC?

Unit Trusts and OEICs are both open ended collective investments and are subject to the same regulation. OEICs became available in May 1997 and were largely introduced as a more flexible alternative to the established industry of Unit Trusts.

An OEIC has an 'Umbrella' fund structure, allowing for many 'sub-funds' with different investment objectives. To the investor this means an easier way to move between different OEICs in the same management group, as there is less administration. OEICs can also offer different share classes for the same fund. This allows for private investors to invest in the same fund as large organisations.

Costs

Unit Trusts and OEICs have an initial charge that is detailed in management group literature or Key Features document. It can sometimes be as much as 6%. So for each £100 invested, around £94 is actually put into the fund. Equity funds tend to have the most expensive initial charge at 5%-6% and Index Trackers and Money Market funds the lowest at 0%-1%. Additionally, there is an annual management charge, which is typically 1-1.5%.

Some funds with low initial charges have a penalty exit fee for short-term investors. This is to encourage people to keep their investment in the fund; the charges decrease the longer the time invested. OEICs have a different charging structure to Unit Trusts. Most funds have different charges for each share class. Institutional shares usually have much lower fees than retail shares due to the greatly increased initial investment into the fund.

Fees often reflect the costs associated with investing in a particular area, so Unit Trust and OEIcs that invest overseas tend to be more expensive than those investing in the UK. It can pay to shop around, as some management companies will be more cost efficient than others.

Pricing

Unit Trusts also price differently to OEICs. Unit Trusts have a bid price (selling price) and an offer price (purchase price). OEICs have a single share price, the mid-market price.

The bid and offer price of a Unit Trust mirrors the value of its investments (known as the Net Asset Value). The initial charge is included in the offer price. As OEICs only have one price, which also reflects the value of its investments, initial charges are shown separately. All shares are bought and sold at the single price.

FAQs

Management companies are happy to answer queries and give help or advice over the phone. They will be able to deal with administrative queries about your fund and other products they provide. Some are prepared to discuss the investment performance of your fund and the current outlook.

How do I invest?
- A Unit Trust or OEIC can be bought through the manager, the company salesman, a stockbroker or a financial advisor.
- For the less experienced investor it is always advisable to go via an authorised independent financial advisor, who can

help you select a fund that suits your needs and also complete all of the transactions on your behalf.

- Once a fund has been chosen contact the management group by telephone, letter or website, if they have one, and ask for an application form.
- Once the company has received your order, units or shares will be purchased at the price calculated according to FSA regulations.
- You will receive a confirmation letter setting out the terms of your request once the order has been placed.
- Any income or dividends generated by the funds investments will be paid to you on set dates.
- If you do not want this income paid to you, you can opt for Accumulation units.
- The income stays in the fund and although you do not receive extra units, the price of your existing units is increased.

What happens after I've invested?

- Once invested you can leave the day-to-day management to the professionals. You should, however, review your portfolio on a regular basis.
- You will be sent a manager's report every six months outlining the progress of your Unit Trust or OEIC.
- Some companies send statements to investors on a yearly basis. These show how many units/shares you hold, any additional investment, re-investment or encashments made since the last

statement, and the latest price of your units/shares.

- If your fund pays out an income, it will do so on fixed dates. You will be sent a notification of income and tax voucher showing how much basic rate tax has been deducted.
- If you own income units, a cheque may accompany the voucher. Otherwise, the income will be paid directly into your bank account or used to buy extra units, depending on the instructions you gave.

How do I monitor performance?

- You can monitor the value of the trust on a daily basis, using the prices published on websites, including TrustNet and in financial papers.
- The prices are calculated at the valuation point on the previous day.
- The prices at which you deal are therefore unlikely to be exactly the same because of market movements.

Can I change from one fund to another?

- As your needs change you may want to change funds.
- You will normally pay an initial charge when purchasing a new fund. Although if you change to a fund under the same company, you may be offered a switching discount.
- Find out the cost of switching beforehand.
- Because of the structure of an OEIC, it is generally easier to switch between OEICs in the same management group.

How can I sell?

- Unit Trusts and OEICs can be cashed in quickly and easily.
- Partial and full encashments are allowed, providing the remaining balance is sufficient to meet the minimum investment requirements.
- You will be given information about how to sell your units/shares when you invest and in the Manager's Reports.
- You can ask your IFA to make the withdrawal for you.
- If you have money in a Cash fund you may be supplied with a chequebook to make withdrawals, but they will have to be relatively large amounts.
- The managers according to the FSA regulations calculate the cash-in value.
- Once your request is received, confirmation will be sent to you and it will take around a week to receive the cheque.

How will I be taxed?

- Unless you are holding your Unit Trust or OEIC within an ISA or PEP, or you are a non-taxpayer, you may be liable to tax on the income and capital gains.
- Any capital gains made within the fund are not taxed and although you are liable to CGT when you cash in the units, you will not have to pay tax if the total gains you make from all your savings in the tax year are within your annual CGT allowance.
- Income from Unit Trusts and OEICs is liable to tax, but the tax is deducted before the income is paid out so basic

rate tax payers will have nothing further to pay. Higher rate taxpayers are liable for extra income tax.

What if things go wrong?

- If you have a complaint go to the management group in the first instance.
- If the management does not satisfactorily answer your query, then speak to the Ombudsman. Contact details can be obtained from the management company or the FSA.
- The Investor's Compensation Scheme will pay up to £48.000 for a valid claim, which is when an authorised business becomes insolvent.

Great site to look at is:
www.trustnet.co.uk you can request a free brochure or read on line.
A big thanks to Paul, I think he has given us a great insight into the subject. Check out the website.

Traded Options

Traded options are not normally suitable for beginners to investing, but I will just give you an insight as to what they are and how they work. It is imperative that you understand completely how they work before you even think about investing in them.

Due to the Nick Leeson affair for those who don't know him (Barings Bank), options have been discussed by the whole of the financial press.
Two commonly traded options are shares and market indices handled by LIFFE (the London International Financial Futures and Options Exchange.)
www.liffe.com the website has a free training course and lots of information available.

I suggest you look at it.

There are two basic types:
Calls and **Puts.**
A **call** is an option to buy a stated number of company's shares at a pre-determined price for a specified period of time.
A **put** is an option to sell a share at a specified price for a specified period of time.

ISAs

ISA stands for Individual Savings Account.
ISAs are savings accounts free of personal taxes that can be used to hold many types of savings and investment products. They have now replaced **Peps** (Personal Equity Plans) and **Tessa's**

ISAs can include one or more of the following components:

* Cash in a bank or building society savings account.
* Life insurance (investment type life insurance policy).
* Stocks and shares (unit trusts, shares, bonds etc).

There are very strict rules regarding the maximum amount allowed that you can invest in any one-tax year.
Any U.K resident over the age of 16 can buy mini cash ISA. Any UK resident over the age of 18 can buy any other sort of ISA. For information on ISAs your bank is a good place to start.
You can also get super information on the different kinds of ISAs and tax benefits by visiting:
www.fsa.gov.uk the site also offer a consumer handbook on different aspects of investing.
Another site that is worth a visit relating to ISAs is www.fairinvestment.com they have a list of ISAs available and a very good explanation of what an ISA actually is and does.
As with everything else be sure to get professional qualified advice.

Lots of people overlook simple investments like rare books, rare wine, rare stamps and works of art. Some antiques can also be a good investment. Of course as in most things you need expert advice, but they are certainly worth looking at.

12

Summary

Well my friends, we are just about at the end and I hope you have enjoyed reading this book as much as I have enjoyed writing it. I have tried to provide a novice investor with the relevant information that will allow him or her to make an informed decision when buying and selling shares. I have never pretended to be an expert and my book is just a good place to start. I have not used a lot of the expert's language for that reason. I couldn't understand it when I started buying shares and I certainly do not understand all of it now.

I am not a qualified trained writer, but I have done my best in ordinary language to help you along your route to financial control.

I hope I have managed to take you from being an ordinary person to a shareholder in a company that will allow your money to grow at a better rate than the bank or building society.

Although I have covered many topics and areas in the book there are no get rich quick schemes when it comes to investing. If there are, I haven't found them.

It's like most things in life; it looks easy until you try it. I thought it would be pretty easy to write this book. What a shock I got. I have nearly driven my family insane. Between the research and the writing and rewriting it has certainly not been an easy task. All be it now I am finished I am very proud of my work. It may not be perfect, but what is?

While I was toying with the design for the front cover of this book, which I completely forgot about I might add.

I decided to sort out a website. Oh! Yes, no problem at all I thought. Not blooming likely. I have no idea if you've ever tried it, but what a nightmare.

I thought I wouldn't bother to pay an expert the £1.000 plus or minus they required for setting it up for me. Well if I count my man-hours trying to do it myself, I would have been cheaper to pay the £1.000. But that's a whole new story.

I have now set up www.osfop.co.uk this is short for "Ordinary Shares for Ordinary People." When you visit the site you will see I have not been very sure what to put on it yet. So I am hoping the people who buy this book will let me know what they would like to see there. Perhaps you want to chat to other novice investors? Perhaps you want to see professional investors information? Perhaps you just want a place to start? Regardless the site is there for you, so just let me know what you want from it and I will do my very best to provide it. Perhaps you want to see my portfolio? Mmmmmm----!!!

For anyone who has ever tried to set up there own website and failed miserably like myself, or just doesn't want to pay £1.000 like myself. You can go to:
www.lipstickwebdesign.com and they will register your domain name, let you choose a professional design for your website. Construct it with 4 pages and host it for a full year, oh and yes they will get you live on the net in no time at all. What do you have to do? Just give them all the information you want on your site, pick your name and design, and sit back. All of this for a very affordable price, at time of going to print.
Sounds too good to be true. Well have a look for yourself. www.lipstickwebdesign.com

You might wonder why you bought this book, now you've discovered there's so much to think about, study and research. Well why do you think there are more than twelve million people in the UK alone currently investing directly in stocks and shares? Yes, you guessed it. They're just the same as you and I, just ordinary people trying to secure their financial future. Well the truth of the matter is the long-term returns on equity investments have still been better than on most alternative investments available to investors. So it's worth all the effort. Especially when you see the reward. I am sure you will.

A few very important points to remember.

* A quick reward can mean a very high risk.
* Over confidence can cost you money.
* Hindsight is a wonderful thing.
* Nobody gets it right all the time.
* Do your homework it pays dividends.
* Be realistic about your goals.
* The only sure thing in this life is death and taxes.

I have read a number of books while researching to write this one. I am not going to list all of them, but here are a few I think will definitely benefit you as a beginner to investing:

The Warren Buffet Way, by Robert G Hagstrom, Jnr.
The neatest little guide to stock market investing, by Jason Kelly.
The Intelligent Investor, by Benjamin Graham.
Common Stocks and Uncommon profits, by Philip Fisher.
Beating the Street, by Peter Lynch.
The Money Masters, by John Train.
The New Market Wizards, by Jack D. Schwager.
Judgement Under Uncertainty, by Daniel Kahnerian and Amos Tversky

All of these books have a great deal to offer. There are many more, but the ones above are a good place to start.

Here are some websites that will definitely benefit you by visiting.

The UK Shareholders Association. They represent smaller shareholders and lobby regulators, governments and companies on their behalf. You will find them at www.uksa.org.uk

APCIMS. The Association of Private Client Investment Managers and Stockbrokers. They are an excellent website for Private Investors. You will find them at www.apcims.org.uk

A few Internet tool sites that offer free charting tools are:

www.moneyam.com
www.advfn.com

A few information sites to check out:

www.market-eye.co.uk
www.iii.co.uk
www.hemscott.net
www.axl.co.uk/Ise
www.sharescope.co.uk
www.moneyguru.co.uk

A few all round good sites for investors:

www.ft.com
www.investorschronicle.co.uk

As you know I have listed a great many Investors websites all through the book. I do not see the point in listing them all again. I have just added a few extra here.

Motley Fool is a very popular website for Shares. The site is not for fools at all but rather for everyone that stands apart from the so-called experts, mainly gurus and talking heads. At this site Wall Streets wise men are foolish and the Motley Fools are wise. Definitely worth a visit. They didn't answer me when I contacted them for advice or tips to novice investors. But we won't hold that against them, now will we? Mmmmm----
www.motleyfool.com

A few American site worth visiting are:

www.marketwatch.com
www.bloomberg.com
www.nyse.com
www.dowjones.com
www.fallstreet.com

www.prudentbear.com
www.financialsense.com
www.cnbc.com

Well I hope you concentrate on the main function of this book.
That is to help you to make your money grow. Don't rush in.
Look at all the relevant websites. Go to the library and pick up
a few of the books. Order a few company reports and read
them.

My husband smiled amusingly yesterday when twelve
company reports turned up on the doorstep. Yes, I will read all
of them, not all at the same time of course.

Follow the steps and conduct your research.

Most importantly, enjoy it. It's good fun. Don't overload
yourself with information. If you feel like that, take a break.
Have a day away from it, if you can. Use the information in the
book to achieve your goal. That is the whole point of the
exercise.

Welcome to the world of Private Investing.

If I can do it anyone can.

If you have any questions or your not sure of anything in the
book. You can contact me through
www.lipstickpublishing.com I'll be more than happy to help
you if I can. If I can't, I will try and find the appropriate person
or expert that can.

Alternately, I will be the mad person behind:
www.osfop.co.uk
So you can contact me there. Email:
admin@osfop.co.uk

If you require further copies of this book you can purchase
them at www.lipstickpublishing.com or www.osfop.co.uk or of
course any good book shop.

So what's left to say? Get out there and enjoy it. I hope I have helped you along the way to financial security. At very least I hope I have put you in control of your financial future.

It's your money. I firmly believe there is no difference whatsoever between an ordinary person and a fat cat. They simply have more knowledge on the subject than most of us.

Well, not any more!!!

Thank you for buying my book.

The End

Yours Sincerely,

Marie Lewis Stevenson.

Website:
www.osfop.co.uk
Email:
admin@osfop.co.uk

Glossary

Advisory broker: A stockbroker who offers investment advice but leaves the final investment decision to the investor.

ACT: Advance Corporation Tax paid by companies on shareholders dividends.

AGM: A company's annual general meeting, held once a year to approve the report and accounts and the final dividend, and vote on any proposed motions.

AIM: The Alternative Investment Market. Launched by the Stock Exchange in 1995 as a market for smaller companies. Aim sets lower standards of entry than the stock exchange official list.

Aftermarket: A collective term for both exchange and over the counter markets, in which stocks are bought and sold after they are first issued. Also known as the secondary market.

Bargain: The stock market term for a share sale or purchase.

Bear: An investor who thinks the market will go down.

Bear Market: A market where the index is falling.

Bid: The price a market maker will pay for a share.

Bid/Offer Spread: The difference between the bid and the offer price.

Blue Chip Companies: Well-established companies with a high market capitalisation.

Bull: An investor who thinks the stock will go up.

Bull Market: A market where the index is rising.

Call: A covered warrant that gives the holder the right, but not the obligation, to buy the underlying investment at a future date and specified price.

Capital Gain: The profit you make between the buying and selling price of shares.

Capital Growth: The rise in the value of your initial investment.

Charting: Capturing the patterns of the overall market or an individual share price on a line, bar or other type of graph.

Commission: The fee charged by a stockbroker for carrying out a customer's instruction to buy or sell.

Consideration: The money value of a transaction (number of shares multiplied by the price) before adding or deducting commission, stamp duty etc.

Crest: The bank of England's new paperless shares settlement system.

Discount: When the market price of a newly issued share is lower than its issue price. The opposite of 'premium'.

Discretionary Broker: A stockbroker who has the discretion to buy shares on an investor's behalf and manage the investor's portfolio.

Dividend: The part of a company's profit which is distributed to shareholders.

Earnings: The net profit of a company that is distributed to shareholders.

Earnings per share (Eps)|: Net profit divided by the number of ordinary shares.

Equity: Basically ordinary shares.

Execution only broker: A stockbroker who merely carries out a transaction on the investor's behalf without offering advice.

Final Dividend: The dividend paid by a company at the end of a financial year.

Flotation: When company's shares are sold to investors and quoted on the stock market for the very first time.

Fundamentals: The underlying financial condition of a company based on its actual earnings, assets and dividends.

Gearing: A company's debt expressed as a percentage of its equal capital. High gearing means its debts are high in relation to capital.

Gross: Before tax has been deducted.

Hedging: Protecting against or limiting losses on an existing shareholding or portfolio by establishing an opposite position in the same or equivalent stock.

Insider dealing: The purchase or sale of shares by someone who possesses 'inside' information about the company. This is information about the company's performance or prospects, which have not yet been made available to the market as a whole, and which if available may affect the share price. In the U.K. this is a criminal offence.

Institutional Investors: Basically, the pension funds and insurance companies who own the majority of quoted shares.

Interim dividend: A dividend declared part way through a company's financial year, authorised solely by the directors.

Liquid: Used to describe a market where there are many buyers and sellers, and consequently it is easy to deal. Investors who hold cash are said to be liquid and those who have sold their holdings have gone liquid.

Market Size: The number of shares in which a market maker is prepared to deal. Either as a buyer or seller.

Merger: The joining of two companies, under either friendly or hostile terms.

Net: After tax has been deducted.

New Issue: Shares coming onto the Stock Exchange for the first time.

Nominal Value: The value ascribed to a share when it is first authorised and issued by a company. It bears no relationship to a shares market value.

Nominee Accounts: An account where a person or company hold shares on behalf of an investor.

Ofex: The unquoted market for smaller companies ran by JP Jenkins.

Penny Shares: Traditionally any shares trading at a low price. Typically less than 20p.

Portfolio: An investor's collection of shares.

Put: A covered warrant that gives the holder the right, but not the obligation, to sell the underlying investment at a future date at a specified price.

Quote: If a company has a quote (or is quoted), its shares can be bought and sold on the stock market.

Registrar: An organisation or an individual that takes responsibility for maintaining a company's share register.

Rights Issue: When an existing plc issues new shares. They are offered to existing shareholders in proportion to their existing holding.

Sectors:	Companies quoted on the London Stock Exchange are subdivided into 40 sectors by industry type.
Settlement:	Once a deal has been made, the settlement process transfers stock from seller to buyer, and arranges corresponding movement of money between both.
Shell:	A moribund company whose main value resides in it's listing on the stock exchange. Commonly taken over by entrepreneurs who inject there own business interests into the company and use the stock market quote to raise equity finance via a series of rights issues or takeover bids.
Spread:	The difference between market makers bid and offer price.
Stamp Duty:	A government tax levied on the purchase of shares. The current rate is 0.5%

Stock Exchange Official list: The main market.Companies that are on the official list have been vetted by the stock exchange Quotations dept and are subject to all the listing rules in the Stock Exchange yellow book.

Stop loss:	A limit placed by an investor on the amount he or she is prepared to lose on an investment.
Volatility:	The relative amount of percentage by which a shares price rises and falls during a period of time.
Volume:	The total number of shares traded in a given period of time.

| Volume: | The total number of shares traded in a given period of time. |
| Warrant: | A long-term option to buy shares. These are offered to existing shareholders initially but can also be traded on the stock market |

Just to add a little further information of help regarding the glossary.

For the definition of any financial term that may not have been covered, or if you come across jargon you don't understand in future studies. Just go and take a look at www.investorschronicle.com Click the word glossary. You can type in any financial word or term here, and an excellent definition will be given. I thought it was simply astounding.

Well my friends this is quite definitely the end of the book and enjoy your investments.

THE END